S0-BDG-956

BRITISH TRADE UNIONISM AGAINST THE TRADES UNION CONGRESS

BRITISH TRADE UNIONISM AGAINST THE TRADES UNION CONGRESS

Gerald A. Dorfman

Hoover Institution Press
Stanford University, Stanford, California

© Gerald A. Dorfman 1983

The Hoover Institution on War, Revolution and Peace, founded at Stanford University in 1919 by the late President Herbert Hoover, is an interdisciplinary research center for advanced study on domestic and international affairs in the twentieth century. The views expressed in its publications are entirely those of the authors and do not necessarily reflect the views of the staff, officers, or Board of Overseers of the Hoover Institution.

Hoover Press Publication 281

ISBN 0--8179--7811--9

Library of Congress Catalog Card Number: 82--83300

Printed in Hong Kong

Contents

Acknowledgements

I wrote this book while a Visiting Scholar at the Hoover Institution at Stanford University. This residence at Hoover was my second, having spent a year there in 1977–8 as a National Fellow. I am therefore very grateful to Hoover for its continuing and generous support. I especially want to thank Dennis Bark, Hoover's Deputy Director, who has always encouraged my work by providing every possible assistance. His secretary, Janet Dutra, has been particularly kind. Senior Fellows Richard Burress, Peter Duignan, Lewis Gann, Alvin Rabushka and Thomas Moore all took an interest in my work and I am grateful to them.

Professor Victor Olorunsola of Iowa State University is a friend and colleague who not only generously encouraged my work but made sacrifices which allowed me to have the time to write this book. I am also grateful to Iowa State University and especially the Iowa State University Research Foundation for providing me with important support for this project.

This study is my third on the Trades Union Congress. Once again, I did all of my research in Britain. Trade union leaders, members of the TUC staff, political leaders and civil servants have been incredibly kind to me during the last dozen years. I regard many of them as close friends and I want them to know how grateful I am for the many interviews and visits which they have hosted.

My family and friends have been wonderful: my parents, Margaret and Ralph Dorfman, Lois and Larry Schwartz; Ben Halpren; and, of course, my children, Lori and Debbie. My wife, Penny, has been terrific as always! Finally, I must thank Polly Tooker, who is a splendid typist, and Audrey Bamber for her excellent index.

G. A. D.

1 The Problem of Trade Union Purpose

1. THE PROBLEM OF UNION–GOVERNMENT RELATIONS IN BRITAIN

The disruptive power of unions in Britain has been painfully obvious in recent years. Strikes have had an impact throughout the society, stopping trains, darkening whole cities and even bringing down governments in dramatic political confrontations. The union movement has seemed at times an impregnable fortress of pressure group power, immune to the legal and political counterforce which Britain's elected leaders have attempted to bring against it.

Scholars have reinforced these images of union power in their analyses of the relationship between unions and government, which they label 'collectivist politics'.[1] They reason that union power originated in the consensus leading politicians fashioned during the Second World War which committed government to manage the economy in order to ensure and protect economic stability. Full employment more than any other aspect of what became a new economic policy endowed the union movement with real strength. Unions suddenly enjoyed significant leverage in wage negotiations and the outcome of those negotiations in turn affected the price competitiveness of British goods on international markets. No wonder, therefore, that British governments became concerned that unions restrain the exercise of their new-found leverage. By their implorings for union cooperation, government drew trade union leaders from the fringes of power into the centre of national economic decision-making.

Several studies have explored union–government relations since the Second World War.[2] Most of them conclude that

1

collectivist politics is a failure; that not only has the union movement resisted government demands for cooperation but that it has struck back to paralyze economic policy. Taking the perspective of 'national interest', they point to Britain's chronic economic distress as the tragic consequence of this process.

The hard data which document Britain's economic performance over the last three decades certainly confirm the bleak result of union–government relations. The national well-being is sorely damaged, and there is no doubt that union intransigence has contributed importantly to this state of affairs.

What has gone relatively unnoticed, however, is that the union movement itself also suffers from the consequencs of its 'victories' over government. High inflation, large numbers of business failures, the fall in the standard of living and political instability, among other things, quite naturally undermine the unions' struggle for the good life. Union leaders are realistic enough to know that they cannot win all of their goals and purposes.[3] They expect to win some, win others partially and lose still others. But their record since the Second World War is surprisingly poor given the influence and power they have supposedly been able to exercise on policy-making. They show only limited progress in real terms toward many goals and virtually no progress toward some others. For example, although higher wages has been a top priority in every year, real wages today are not significantly higher than they were several dozen years ago.[4] Likewise, the vital goal of full employment which seemed so securely achieved during the 1940s and 1950s has steadily slipped away in recent years.[5] And progress towards industrial democracy, also a long-proclaimed union goal, has been very slight. In fact, trade unions today even face the prospect of losing the very collectivist process which endowed them with significant power in the first place.

A major question for this study to answer is why and how did the trade union movement fail to better use the opportunities which collectivist politics gave them to influence policy-making in an advantageous direction? In looking for answers, this study concentrates on the work of the Trades Union Congress (TUC). The TUC is the centralized union authority and as such is responsible for seeking and winning the national elements of trade union purpose. It conducts relations with all institutions of government including stewardship of union participation in collectivist politics. This means that the strategy and tactics of relations with government are formulated within its decision-making structures by the interaction of individual union leaders, the TUC General Secretary and the TUC permanent staff.

2. POLITICS AT THE TRADES UNION CONGRESS

This study starts with the view that the TUC suffers from its construction as a loose federation. Such an arrangement posed no problems for union interests so long as government remained primarily an observer of economic activity. But once government took command of the economy the Trade Union Congress sorely needed sufficient authority to negotiate with national leaders about the terms of economic policy.

It was at that point, however, that constituent unions made it clear that they had different ideas. They had urged government to take control of the economy in order to create and then protect full employment and a 'decent' standard of living. They were also anxious that the TUC work to press these purposes, while protecting them from other government policies – such as wage restraint – which they found threatening. Yet, they were distinctly unwilling to contribute permanent shares of their own authority and prerogatives to the cause. They firmly rejected any notion of a strong general staff for labour which might respond coherently to the demands of collectivist politics.

The consequence of this jealous attitude impinges at the heart of this study. The Trades Union Congress has constantly been unequal to the collectivist relationship it encouraged. Government management of the economy persistently and inevitably intrudes, requiring TUC responses at some points, and encouraging union interest in winning positive influence at others. The problem for trade unionism is that each new policy demand, whether positive or negative, calls up a new round of contention about the distribution of power between individual unions and the TUC. This repetitive process in turn further undermines the effectiveness of TUC leadership. It divides and debilitates the TUC's executive body of individual union leaders, the General Council, as well as the leadership of the TUC General Secretary and his staff. Decision-making at the TUC is therefore a destructively political exercise, whose outcome is often more relevant to the continuing arguments within the organization than to the substantive issues which trade unionism hopes to influence. Little wonder then that TUC response to government is crudely intransigent, even though usually damaging to union purpose.

3. THE ORIGINS OF TUC WEAKNESS

The TUC has been relatively ineffective in achieving union goals in great part because of decisions taken about its power during a few crucial years between the end of the First World War and the General Strike of 1926. It was during that time that its constituent unions considered, tried and then rejected the creation of a true 'general staff for labour'.[6] The circumstances leading to their decision virtually insured that similar proposals for greater TUC power would be rejected in later years. Thus, the Trades Union Congress was forced to interact over the years with an increasingly powerful government but without the authority to make its interaction fully effective. The contradiction in this situation was that its member unions no less than the British government and British society expected and wanted the Trades Union Congress to participate in this collectivist process as if it *had been given* real power and authority.

National trade unionism and the Trades Union Congress itself were not significant before the First World War. The main focus of union activity was on the shop floor within individual factories before 1914. The TUC functioned sporadically, coming to life during the annual Congress, when its Parliamentary Committee met from time to time as the ongoing directing authority and for brief periods when national issues greatly threatened broad union interests.

Change from this pattern began during the War. Government gradually took control of the economy for the first time. Major labour problems accordingly became more national and their solutions depended on the development of a continuous relationship between the government and a national trade union centre. Wages and prices as well as the administration of some industries which government took into its control became the major subjects of interaction.

Although the Government did reduce the level of its intervention once the war had ended, the nature of economic relationships remained permanently changed. Government simply could not return to its previous disinterest. Industrial concentration had produced much more national economic activity and control. This development, in turn, created the need for both larger and more powerful national trade unions and a national union centre capable of effectively dealing with government on a full-time basis.

The development of a stronger TUC to act as a national union spokesgroup was slower and far more painful, however, than the external situation dictated. The major problem was that national union leaders were largely in disrepute with their members. They had been slow to understand and take advantage of the enormous increase in union leverage which was produced by the needs of all-out wartime production. The rank and file, led by militant shop stewards in the factories, had complained bitterly during the war years that their leaders were simply ignoring obvious bargaining advantages. For example, while demand-inflation pushed prices ever higher in 1916 and 1917, national union leaders had continued to refuse to press the government for a more generous wages policy. Shop stewards thereupon took matters into their own hands by declaring unofficial (wildcat) strikes in order to press their popular demands. The force of their rebellion was pointedly demonstrated by a doubling of the number of days lost to strikes between 1915 and 1917.[7]

The Coalition Government ultimately felt compelled to give in to shop stewards' demands. It relaxed procedures for granting wage increases, restrained food prices and added several important union leaders to administrative positions within the Government. This helped to ameliorate the situation but in the process gave the rank and file as well as their shop stewards a considerable victory at the expense of national union leaders.

Once the war ended, this same national union leadership struggled for some time to overcome their disability. In order to reassert their authority, they concentrated on re-establishing power within their own unions and tried to do so by exploiting a strong, though short-lived, economic boom. Their strategy was to convert their cautious and conservative wartime approach into a much more militant stance which included an uninhibited willingness to use the strike weapon. The enormous surge in the number of strikes and particularly the number of workers involved testified to the consequences of their new behaviour.

This explosion of industrial conflict did produce a number of large settlements while it helped to re-establish the credibility of many tarnished union leaders. But it fell short of winning the kinds of permanent improvements, such as in the conditions of work, which it had promised to achieve. It became painfully obvious during 1918 and 1919 that uncoordinated and unthinking militáncy had accomplished much less for each union than might have been gained by a more collective or at least a more coordinated effort.

This realization did much finally to launch real efforts to create a stróng directing authority at the trade union centre, the TUC. It was, however, ironic and unfortunate for union interests and later for larger government interests that this move occurred as good economic conditions dissolved rapidly into a recession which was not to end for twenty years. What therefore started as a move to centralize union politics in order to better exploit and control the advantages of improved bargaining leverage was used instead to try to forestall the savage consequences of reduced leverage. It was to be a bad context in which a more powerfully endowed TUC tried to earn its credibility.

The specific trigger for reforming the TUC emerged out of the settlement of the rail strike in 1919.[8] Ernest Bevin, the leader of the Transport Union, proposed that the functions of the Mediation Committee which had so successfully intervened in the rail strike, should be applied to the TUC itself.[9] He suggested that the chaotic and unrewarding experiences of the previous few years had demonstrated that the union movement now needed permanent machinery for coordinating and mediating industrial actions.

Taking this cue, the Parliamentary Committee of the TUC subsequently appointed a Coordination Committee to explore the feasibility of Bevin's proposal. The Committee completed its work during 1920. It recommended, and Congress that year accepted, a significant programme of reform.[10] The Parliamentary Committee was enlarged, made more representative, and renamed the General Council. In turn, the Council was authorized to employ a full-time TUC staff to administer a whole range of new functions. It was to coordinate industrial actions of all kinds, to help settle inter-union disputes, to speak for the industrial side of the labour movement with government at all levels of jurisdiction and to be responsible for relations with international trade unionism.

These changes created the form of a strong trade union centre. They did not, however, create the power. The General Council was endowed with this long list of responsibilities but its ablity to take decisive action on any of them was sharply limited by its need to enlist the cooperation of its constituent member unions. Like the Parliamentary Committee before it, the new Council could do no more than persuade. It thus depended on the will of each member union on each issue. And the long history of the TUC to that point clearly showed that member unions would only reluctantly surrender portions of their authority to the collective and then only when they believed that the collective would either enhance or protect their *particular* interests.

The 'new' Trades Union Congress which emerged from these reforms was thus much more highly developed and prepared to consider and represent the union movement on the great issues of the day even if it could not take powerful action itself. Had the boom of the early postwar years continued, it might have been possible for the TUC gradually to have gained significant additional powers by demonstrating its skilful leadership.

The critical and threatening events of the following four years, from 1921 to 1925, made this speculation and the potential for gradualism impossible to fulfill. The sudden decline in Britain's economic fortunes put a quite different stress on the role of the TUC. It sharpened the argument about what powers and responsibilities the TUC should have. Whereas these questions might have been debated peacefully over a number of years while the TUC demonstrated its potential, the issues at such a crisis moment became inflamed and immediate. Should the newly revamped and apparently more capable TUC take on the responsiblity for defending union interests against the attacks which recession was provoking employers to make? With the memories of powerful but uncoordinated postwar strikes so fresh, the potential for using the new TUC leadership became irresistible.

Congress at first defeated efforts to bolster TUC power during the early 1920s, reaffirming each time the traditional reluctance which had underpinned the reform itself.[11] However by 1924 and 1925, there was a 'distinct shift to the Left',[12] both on the General Council and at the Annual Congress. 'Impatience of the continued high level of unemployment may well have been

responsible for this shift. . . .' 'There was also the experience of
the first Labour Government, which held office during 1924. For
many this was a disillusioning experience, . . .'[13] because the
Government failed to take any significant action to solve or even
relieve the unemployment problem.[14] Ramsey Macdonald and his
Labour colleagues did not, in fact, seem any different in office
than their Tory and Liberal predecessors. This perception
strengthened 'the hand of those who had long argued that wage
earners must rely primarily upon their direct industrial power,
rather than Parliamentary pressure, . . .'[15] to protect their
interests.

The 1924 TUC Congress was the first which showed how
strongly these sentiments were reverberating within the union
movement. Such radical leaders as Arthur Cook of the Miners
and Alonzo Swales of the Engineering Union, who had rejected
collaboration with Labour and instead called for the use of direct
industrial power gained a majority on the General Council. Most
importantly, they used their strength immediately to win new
power for the Council which for the first time gave the TUC the
ability to lead significant conflict. A General Council information
pamphlet published shortly after the 1924 Hull Congress best
describes the terms and significance of this change:

At the Hull Congress in 1924, the duties of the General
Congress were considerably extended. The obligation was
definitely imposed upon Unions to keep the General Council
informed on industrial matters, particularly those which
involve large bodies of workers. The General Council was
given power to intervene in a dispute when negotiations had
failed and where large bodies of workers were involved; or
where standards of wages, hours or conditions of employment
were imperilled. In such cases, the Council was given the
initiative of calling the Unions into consultation and using its
influence to effect a just settlement. In general, however, the
Council is not to intervene where there is any prospect
whatever of the difference being amicably settled, except, of
course, at the request of the Unions concerned. Where the
Council does intervene and its assistance is accepted,
and where, despite the efforts of the Council, a stoppage
of work is enforced by the policy of employers, the Council
must organize all such moral and material support for the

Unions as the circumstances of the dispute appear to justify.[16]

It was this remarkable increase in power which the TUC used to lead the fateful General Strike eighteen months later in support of the Miners Union.

The General Strike has been well described elsewhere.[17] Its importance for this discussion is that its conduct gave a black eye to the concept of powerful TUC leadership. Conflict is not inexorably linked with a strong directing trade union centre, but the course of events in 1926 created such a link in the psyche of British trade unionism. It is this link more than any other factor which has undermined efforts to recreate the sort of 'general staff for labour' which the TUC was developing in 1924 and 1925. Moderate as well as radical elements came to agree that: (1) the TUC should not have strong, formal power to dictate to its constitute unions, but instead should continue to depend upon the willingness of individual unions to cooperate on each issue, and (2) that trade unionism should avoid the use of direct industrial confrontation in the future, and instead should work through the political system to effect change.

This one, very brief exercise in TUC power thus aborted both the immediate development of a directing authority as well as the long-term and gradual development of such strength. Yet, the cogent arguments which Ernest Bevin had used a half dozen years earlier to promote the idea of a significant trade union centre were still relevant and were to be even more so in the future. Government involvement in the economy and increasingly larger and more centralized industrial production and decision-making made the consequent need to coordinate union behaviour more not less important. Boom had been replaced by recession but the nature of the argument for centralized union leadership could be made as compelling in either case.

This point was certainly not lost on the TUC leadership as it struggled in 1927 to recover from the General Strike. Ernest Bevin teamed up with Walter Citrine, the TUC General Secretary, to fashion a new approach. Citrine defined their views as well as the nature of his collaboration with Bevin in his autobiography, *Men and Work:*

The principal lesson I had learned was that the trade union movement must exert its influence in an ever-widening sphere and not be contained within the traditional walls of trade union policy. Events were moving fast and the widely held belief in the impending collapse of capitalism would not suffice. We must try to expand the activities of the T.U.C. until we could establish an efficient system whereby the T.U.C. would be regularly and naturally consulted by whatever Government was in power on any subject of direct concern to the unions. I reasoned that this was a policy to be advocated whenever I got the chance. So, almost without realizing it, I found myself evolving a twofold policy, the parts of which were interdependent. The first led towards more power to the T.U.C., and the second was a demand for consultation in the widest area of economic and industrial policy.[18]

The Citrine–Bevin approach was pragmatic. It was an effort to finesse the consequences of the General Strike which threatened to destroy TUC influence on national policy-making as well as its ability to lead the trade union movement. The two men urged that the TUC drop its attention to conflict and confrontation. Instead, they insisted that the TUC should develop its own capability to understand and express its views on current industrial, economic, social and political problems, with the purpose of carving out trade unionism's place in the capitalist system's decision-making process. By doing so, they also hoped to overcome the now fierce resistance of both moderate and radical leaders to TUC leadership. The TUC would return to its traditional dependence on the voluntary cooperation of its constituent unions but, they reasoned, would be in a far better position to win that cooperation because its new and close relationship with Government would cause constituent unions to look for help and 'protection' from the trade union centre.

The history of Britain's economic and political development after 1926 demonstrate how well the Bevin–Citrine strategy worked on one level and failed miserably on the other. The circumstances leading to government's adoption of the social and economic contract of 1944 could not have been better for yielding access and influence for the trade union movement and the TUC in particular. Government management of the economy with full employment as its linchpin were perfect stimulants which caused the political leadership of both parties to draw unionism from the fringes of power into the closet of negotiations and even bargaining. Yet, throughout this development the pace of a parallel increase in TUC power *vis-à-vis* its constituent member unions was much slower. Contrary to Citrine and Bevin's hopes and expectations individual unions were anxious to enlist TUC protection very readily but unwilling to 'pay' more than temporary, fleeting or superficial contributions of their own prerogatives. As a result, the TUC's growth as an effective spokesgroup for the union movement remained stunted. The consequences of this faulted development have been, of course, tragic for Britain's economic and political life.

4. CONSEQUENCES OF TUC WEAKNESS

Wage politics has been the great battleground on which the Citrine–Bevin strategy has been most severely tested.[19] No issue has been more crucial to union–government relations and to each side's own interests. Government, for its part, came to need union cooperation in exercising wage restraint as an inevitable consequence of its management of the economy. Unions in turn were required to address this issue which more than any other matter touches the very essence of union purpose. Wage politics thus became the cornerstone for a broad gauged interaction in which the Trades Union Congress sought to gain the greatest possible access and influence on policy, while government sought the greatest possible cooperation, advice and acquiescence from the unions.

The actual course of the TUC's performance has been mixed. It won access and influence because full employment after 1945 created pressure for higher wages which put the TUC into a crucial bargaining position with government. Yet its influence was almost entirely negative. It could paralyse and even veto government policies it did not like but it could only rarely influence government to adopt alternatives which it suggested or endorsed. The problem for the TUC as a chief spokesgroup for trade unionism was that government demands for wage restraint stirred resistance by individual unions. This in turn had the effect of reinforcing the inclination of these individual unions jealously to harbour their prerogatives and consequently to deny power to the TUC. Thus, as governments demanded more cooperation the TUC became less rather than more powerful and in the process revealed the fundamental weakness which Citrine and Bevin had hoped to finesse.

The history of collectivist politics in Britain since 1945 illustrates this process and its consequences with painful vividness. Both Labour and Conservative governments repeatedly bid for union cooperation. The TUC response varied depending on the party in office, the economic circumstances at the time and the nature of internal union politics. But the overall record was that the TUC, with a few exceptions, either would not or could not deliver its cooperation even though the consequences of their refusal reverberated against important union interests.

Looking at the historical experience more closely, it is possible to conclude that the TUC's reaction to government demands for cooperation in restraining wages have depended *most* on which party was in office. There have been six clear 'wage politics' episodes since the end of the Second World War: 1947–8, 1956, 1961, 1964–7, 1972–4, and 1976–9.[20] Labour governments initiated half of these, in 1947–48, 1964–7, and 1976–79. Conservative governments initiated the other half: in 1956, 1961–3, and most recently in 1972–4. The difference in these experiences relates most strongly to the familial ties between a Labour government and the trade union movement and the explicitly hostile relations between Conservatives and trade unionists.

Labour governments accordingly have been able quite frequently to use their fraternal ties to goad a reluctant TUC into agreeing to wage restraint, often without making substantial concessions to trade union interests. But these restraints have been either short-lived or sabotaged immediately by disobedient rank and file members on the shop floor. Conservative governments, by contrast, have run into traditional union distrust and hostility which cause the TUC easily to reject their wage restraint overtures. In either case, the ultimate outcomes have been the failure of incomes policy.

This whole process thus exposed the TUC's fundamental weakness while it paralyzed collectivist politics in Britain. In many of these episodes even the TUC staff and its leadership were in favour of union cooperation. They reasoned that incomes policies made good economic sense and moreover that 'sensible' cooperation with government of either party would improve the TUC's bargaining ability to win concessions in favour of other union policy interests. But matters have never been very much in their control and instead of cooperation the TUC delivered policy vetoes and policy stalemate – or watched as they were delivered by the membership in the organization below.

(i) The example of the ineffective alliance with Labour, 1964–7

The course of the bargaining between the Wilson Government and the TUC between 1964 and 1967 about wage restraint well illustrates the TUC's internal dilemma. The TUC General Secretary, the TUC staff, and a majority on the General Council were agreed that the success of the Wilson Government depended in great measure on the cooperation of the trade union movement in keeping wage rises more or less equivalent to rises in industrial productivity.[21] They were willing to convert this view into a workable incomes policy if the Government would carefully take into account the counterforce against wage restraint which was simmering on the shop floor. George Woodcock, the TUC General Secretary, expressed this problem in a call for a gradual approach. Woodcock was personally keen on incomes policy but he fervently believed that it could work only if trade unionists had enough time to 'learn' that wage restraint was really in their interests and enough time to adjust to its consequences in their pay packets.[22] Putting it another way, Woodcock on a number of occasions frankly admitted that the Trades Union Congress did not have the power on its own to impose incomes policy on its membership and could not negotiate in good faith with government in a way which implied that they did have such authority.

The Labour Government understood Woodcock's caution but it also recognized the force of other pressures to impose an immediate wage restraint. Using the advantage of its familial ties with organized labour, the Wilson Government in 1964 gambled that it could pressure a reluctant TUC into an immediate incomes policy which its leadership could in turn enforce on the rank and file. In particular, George Brown, the Minister for Economic Affairs, had reasoned that he could use his personal relations with members of the General Council to overcome their reluctance.[23] He refused to accept George Woodcock's caution about the limited ability of the TUC to impose such a policy against the will of its members and particularly against the will of the now-powerful shop stewards movement. But, in fact, Woodcock proved to be quite prescient. A majority on the General Council did reluctantly honour their personal friendships with Brown and their loyalty to the Labour Government by reaching a wage restraint agreement. But that agreement proved worthless as it was destroyed in local plant level bargaining during the course of the following year and a half.

The real outcome of the collectivist relationship during those years was thus policy sabotage. The Government got its agreement but in the end the agreement was worthless and wages continued to rise in the same destructive pattern. Ultimately, the Wilson Government in 1966 decided to legislatively impose rather than negotiate its wages policy, giving only symbolic value to later talks. By 1967 the TUC was effectively shut out of important influence on Government policies while at the same time subject to the statutory restraints on wage rises which its rank and file had vetoed earlier.

5. THE FAILED COUNTERATTACK AGAINST UNION POWER, 1968–74

This example is but one of many such episodes during the decades after 1945. In every case, both the Government's policy intentions and union interests were damaged by the failure of collectivist politics to work. By the late sixties, leaders of both parties began to question whether this paralyzing struggle between the political system and the trade union movement could be 'allowed' to continue to wreak such havoc.

By 1968, the Labour Government as well as its Tory opposition decided separately to fight back. Industrial relations was the key issue which sparked this decision. Political leaders worried that the rising tide of strikes posed a significant and unacceptable threat to their authority. The Wilson Government and subsequently the Heath Government staged counterattacks against union power, with the goal of wrestling back the advantage.

Both efforts failed miserably between 1968 and 1974. The Wilson Government, beginning in 1968, tried to legislate restraints on militant behaviour and especially the use of unofficial strikes. Their purpose was to restore the authority of union leaders which, in turn, they hoped would encourage these leaders to accept familial pressure for cooperation.[24]

Edward Heath's Government beginning in mid-1970 tried an entirely different strategy. Accepting that it suffered an inherently bad relationship with the union movement, the Heath Government sought to develop a new framework of industrial relations law as well as an economic policy which would put the relationship on 'automatic pilot'.[25] The plan was that the law would be enforced by the courts and thus constrain industrial misbehaviour without political intervention. Their economic policy would simultaneously operate without the need of continuous consultation, advice and, ultimately, great doses of cooperation.

The failure of each strategy occurred in different ways but each fell victim to the negative union power they were designed to weaken. The fatal flaw in each government's strategy was that they avoided directly attacking the real basis of union power. They did nothing to renounce or even significantly alter the manner of their management of the economy, including the long-standing commitment to maintain full employment. Political leaders well understood that full employment especially was the linchpin of union power but they were afraid to tamper with what seemed an inviolable guarantee.[26] They worried quite simply that they would pay an awful price at the election polls and thus suffer the same fate that Winston Churchill did in 1945.

6. THE BEGINNING OF THE END OF COLLECTIVIST POLITICS

The defeat of the Heath Government in the chaos of the Miners' strike of 1973–4 marked the end of the purposeful counter attacks against union power. The TUC emerged from these struggles more rather than less influential with government. The return of Labour to office in February 1974 in fact opened a unique period lasting about a year and a half during which the TUC finally gained constant and important positive influence over the terms of public policy. It was an unprecedented time marked by open debate about whether the influence of unions in Whitehall had become overbearing.[27]

It was therefore quite ironic that at this moment of supreme union influence, the most potent economic calamity of the postwar era struck Britain in a way which finally delivered a real challenge to that influence. Recession almost perversely came to the rescue of Britain's battered political elite. Hyperinflation, falling industrial production and financial crisis all operated to undermine union power. They worked so effectively because they undermined the long-standing Keynesian theories which underpinned the economic and social commitment which were made in 1944. Full employment in particular began to slip away in 1975. A Labour Government, no less, began gradually and 'reluctantly' to administer a very different kind of economic management.

This change produced a watershed in British politics. As the underpinnings of union power ebbed after 1975 the basis on which unions demanded and won their place in national economic decision-making began to diminish. The awesome power to provoke industrial disruption remained very potent, but soaring unemployment clearly defused considerable militancy. It would be rash to conclude that this process immediately ended the collectivist era which had then lasted thirty years, but it significantly changed the relationship in a way which improved government leverage. It opened up the real possibility therefore that over time collectivist politics might well disappear or change into a form which would be unrecognizable from the pattern during the first three decades.

The most significant clues about what direction this change will take were offered during the last half of the seventies and the early years of the 1980s. One point is already becoming quite clear. The weakness and confusion of the Trades Union Congress in its role as the central spokesgroup for trade unionism will be more intense. What Citrine and Bevin had tried to finesse fifty years ago remains its most salient problem. Faced with an emerging post-collectivist era in which it is denied a place at the centre of decision-making, the TUC will be even less able to defend and promote trade union purpose. Jealous member unions will find that even the defensive strength offered by the TUC will be unequal to the protection which they will want to enlist.

This study explores the behaviour of the Trades Union Congress at the beginning of this new era. It examines just how the TUC works, taking and implementing decisions which as much as possible attempt to compensate for its inherent weakness. And it explores how the TUC has reacted to the decline of its access and influence on national political decision-making.

(i) Decision-making structures at the Trades Union Congress

The decision-making process and organizational structure within the TUC demonstrates how the union centre expresses and attempts to come to terms with its congenital weakness. Its challenge is to forge workable policies which maximize its effectiveness as a pressure group. Union leaders tenaciously guard their individual prerogatives but at the same time hold a considerable stake in supporting a TUC which is at least effective enough to protect their individual interests on the national level. In practice, this means that constituent unions do what they can within a limited framework to concentrate and focus decision-making and implementation within the TUC as much as possible.

For this very practical reason, the TUC functions more smoothly and efficiently when dealing with routine business than its debilitating federal structure might predict. Deference is the key to its limited success. Junior members of the General Council defer to the leadership of an interlocking directorate of senior colleagues, the TUC staff and especially the TUC General Secretary. This means that on a day-to-day basis the Trades Union Congress is able to state and press its views with government quite coherently and without significant fear of repudiation by individual union leaders who hold near veto power.

It is, of course, in the more stressful and crucial situations that the fragility of TUC government is demonstrated. At those moments, the interlocking directorate needs carefully to seek authority to represent the interests of its individual union constituents. Persuasion and elaborate politics become the order of the day when senior union leaders plunge into important negotiating sessions with ministers. TUC leaders go all out to press the levers of socialization, ambition and even intimidation to win the acquiescence of their colleagues, however fleeting such grants of authority might be.

The record of this intra-union politics has been as good as could be expected, but obviously unsuccessful in important terms.

Having failed to capitalize on the opportunities which collectivist politics provided, the TUC as an organization is hardly ready to fight back now against a new post-Keynesian relationship in which it is more excluded from the decision-making process.

(ii) The politics of failure: the 'winter of discontent,' 1978–79

The last years of the Callaghan Government provided the initial test of TUC behaviour in this new context of post-Keynesian economic management. Full employment had long provided the leverage for TUC power which at least helped to mask the TUC's congenital internal weakness. But after 1976 the TUC had watched almost helplessly as unemployment lines grew and as government gradually abandoned the other commitments of the 1944 economic and social contract.

The dilemma caused by this situation was that the inherently weak, and now even weaker, TUC came under greater rather than less pressure to work as an effective producer group. This demand came from two important directions and was destructively contradictory in each case. For its part , the Labour Government continued to demand 'fraternal' cooperation in restraining rises in wage rates as well as cooperation on the full range of its economic policies. It behaved, in fact, as if nothing had changed since the early days of the 1974 Wilson Government when the relationship produced a stream of policy benefits for trade unionism. In 1978 the Government made its demands for cooperation just as it always had but offered nothing in return which the TUC could hold up to its membership as examples of worthwhile trade-offs for their sacrifice.

At the same time, individual unions treated the TUC with similarly contradictory demands. They insisted, on the one hand, that the TUC become more aggressive and effective in defending their interests against the Government's new economic policies and especially the rise in unemployment. Yet, these same demanding unions had become so suspicious of the Government's intentions and the TUC's weakness that they were even more reluctant than usual to defer to the TUC leadership which they wanted otherwise to invoke.

The best example of this dilemma was the negotiations in the autumn of 1978 between the TUC and ministers about the future course of the government's economic policies. The established governing process within Congress House involves concentrating authority for bargaining purposes in the hands of a few senior union leaders and the General Secretary. This small group is careful to regularly consult their General Council colleagues as well as to remain within prescribed policy limits. However, within these constraints, the small group of elders has always been able to count on a free reign both to conclude agreements and then to have the endorsement of a vast majority of the General Council. This process doesn't create strong TUC government but it has created stable, predictable and at least somewhat effective government.

Matters in 1978, however, proceeded to an unprecedented outcome. The actual negotiations were especially difficult because senior TUC leaders were sensitive to the deteriorating milieu in which they were functioning. They wanted to help the Government but they especially wanted to protect union interests as thoroughly as possible. Wage restraint was not to be part of this agreement because it was well known that the rank and file were in no mood for another year of prescribed wage increases. Thus, the final agreement was tortuously reached and stated no more than a minimum and vague understanding that both sides were to work together. Nonetheless, the General Council on a tie vote defeated the proposal even though it had the explicit support of the Economic Committee.

This was a jarring and unprecedented decision within the TUC, and it undoubtedly contributed to the weakness of its leadership in the chaos of industrial relations during the following months. The two sides ultimately reached a new agreement in February 1979, but not until matters were at the crisis point during the 'winter of discontent'. Familial relations thus still operated between the two sides of the labour movement when survival was at stake. But there was no hiding the weakness and ineffectiveness of the TUC in the new conditions at the end of the 1970s.

(iii) The politics of continuing failure: the beginning of the Thatcher Government, 1979–80

The election of Mrs Thatcher's Conservative Government in May 1979 plunged Trades Union Congress officials into despair.

They were depressed that the 'winter of discontent' had so obviously contributed to her victory and they despaired at the prospects which her Government offered for union interests. They had no doubts whatsoever that she would faithfully carry out her commitments to exclude trade unionism from public policymaking and worse they despaired that she would succeed in this purpose.

The first weeks and months of the new Government's incumbency showed that these concerns were well founded. Mrs Thatcher and her economic and industrial ministers moved aggressively and with considerable political skill to impose their policies. They used their obvious political leverage over trade unionism with great success. Sir Geoffrey Howe, for example, proceeded to design and implement the most signficant change in economic policy in thirty-five years without so much as consulting with nor considering trade union views. The TUC stood by helpless as their demands for attention went unheeded and later as their demands for reconsideration were ignored. When they finally did succeed in meeting with the Chancellor and the Prime Minister, they suffered the even greater indignity of being unable to present their views as Mrs Thatcher monopolized the meeting by her delivery of a sharp lecture on the virtues of monetarist economics.

The TUC had greater success in the area of industrial relations, but even there the outcome was successful in a very limited and defensive way. Jim Prior, the Employment Secretary, did prove agreeable to TUC negotiations and ultimately to their cooperation in fending off hardline Tory backbenchers who wanted more punitive legislation. But Prior's legislation was quite mild and certainly a pale sequel to the earlier Industrial Relations Act. TUC success in influencing Prior was therefore not very impressive, especially if it is viewed as a strategic deflection by Tory leaders who were far more anxious to win unopposed implementation of their economic policies.

Whatever the outcome of Mrs Thatcher's incumbency, its beginnings were important because they established that a new collectivist relationship is in place. The old Tory disadvantage of a cold and distant relationship with the union movement has turned into an asset. The weakening force of post-Keynesian economic policies on union power, especially that of high unemployment, were imposing a distinct influence. Even more than their Labour predecessors, the Tories can now operate their own policies without suffering the impossible costs of bidding for union cooperation. The outcome of Mrs Thatcher's policies therefore depend much more than any postwar government on their merits, and thus much less on the quality of union–government interaction. This point will certainly not be lost on future governments – whatever their political stripe or ideological inclination.

(iv) Post-collectivist politics

These examples of the 'winter of discontent' and the beginning of the Thatcher Government demonstrated the likely outlines of post collectivist politics in Britain. They indicate that the trade union movement and government will continue to find their relationship very important. But they also show that continuing high levels of unemployment will endow government with a decided advantage. A weakening trade union movement will therefore almost certainly want and need to create a much stronger Trades Union Congress to effectively promote and defend its interests, which will be under great stress.

This study offers a modest proposal with this goal in mind. It takes into account traditional union resistance to structural and other rule changes. Instead, it suggests that the TUC might gain power indirectly and over time by gradually creating a closer *interdependence* with its constituent members. The specific approach would be to draw leaders and their unions into a much more direct and continuing involvement with the business of national trade unionism at the TUC.

2 Decision-making Structures at the Trades Union Congress

How the union movement behaves as a pressure group in Britain is the product of its own 'government', the Trades Union Congress. The failure of collectivist politics with its dire consequences both for Britain's economic performance as well as the purpose of trade unionism itself is part of the record of that 'government'. In trying to understand why it behaves as it does, it is obviously important to know how the TUC is organized and how it makes its policy decisions.

The fact that the Trades Union Congress is a federal government means that it draws its power and authority from its member unions. How much power it should have and how it should be able to use that power have always been the subject of heated disagreement within the trade union movement. The answer has usually been 'as little power as possible' so that the primary goal of TUC work has been to overcome as best it could its congenital and self-destructive weakness.

Constituent unions have always zealously guarded their independence. They are strongly in favour of the work of the Trades Union Congress but only so far as it protects interests beyond their reach and does so without too much cost to their prerogatives. Before the days of strong interventionist government, the Trades Union Congress fits this model very well, and member unions could turn its processes on and off at will. Once the government became much more domineering, aggressive and pervasive, individual unions faced a serious dilemma about how their central union government, the TUC, should operate.

The irony of this change and its resulting dilemma was that the union movement itself was a prime force encouraging the development of strong, interventionist government. Its view was that the well-being of working people would be considerably enhanced by public policies which sought to ensure full employment and a 'decent' and rising standard of living as well as the other elements of a better life. And as part of this change, the union movement also envisioned its strong and continuous participation in national public policy-making in a way which the TUC had never experienced before.

The problem though was that the Trades Union Congress needed considerably greater authority in order to carry out this new responsibility. Individual unions were eager to participate in the new economic order, but they held fast to their traditional stubborness and refused to recognize the power requirements of the new situation. They wanted instead to decide as they always had on an *ad hoc* and totally voluntary basis what contributions to make.

It has been just this formula which has not worked during the last three and one-half decades of the collectivist era. The problem has persistently been that each policy issue generates debilitating arguments about the distribution of power between constituent unions and the TUC. Individual unions to this day continue to worry that collective authority operating on a permanent and continuous basis will work against their own interests.

This means that decision-making at the TUC is persistently fraught with considerable danger for the viability of the organization. It also means that TUC leaders must work constantly to overcome their organizational weakness in order to produce reasonably effective union government.

The structure and decision-making processes at the TUC express and attempt to come to terms with this situation. Even though union leaders continue to jealously guard their individual power, they do recognize that they have a considerable stake in supporting a TUC which can protect their interests on the national level. This has meant in practical terms that union leaders have been willing, within a limited framework, to allow a high degree of concentrated and focused authority within the TUC. They have accordingly created an interlocking directorate which leads its work.

This directorate includes six union leaders who together serve on the TUC's most important committees: the General Purpose and Finance, the Economic, and the International. On the staff side, it includes one Deputy and two Assistant General Secretaries as well as the heads or Secretaries of the Economic and International and, at times, the Organization departments. And above all, it includes the General Secretary who is the formal spokesperson for the TUC.

The answers to two key questions will throw considerable light on the TUC's decision-making process. How do members of these three distinct elements gain and hold their power? How do they interact to decide policy and thereby exercise the power and influence of the TUC?

1. THE UNION LEADERS

The major instrument for participation by union leaders in the work of the TUC is the General Council.[1] The Council is formally the great peak of continuing national union authority, replacing the TUC Congress in between its annual week-long sessions.[2] Theoretically, the General Council dominates and the General Secretary and his staff serve its wishes. In practice, the General Council is a vital decision-making force only when the most contentious and crisis-ridden issues are at stake. At other times, the General Council restrains its behaviour, hearing and endorsing the reports of its committees and its senior leadership.

Members of the Council who are not part of the senior inner circle of powerful union leaders content themselves with the knowledge that their deference has rewards in both personal and institutional terms. They recognize that a highly focused leadership produces the best possible, if not perfect, influence for the TUC. They know that they have reserved the right at all times to reassert the authority of their individual unions. And they also know that the seniority system within the Council will yield a position of influence for them if they can serve a sufficiently long term. Moreover, they enjoy the national attention they receive, along with the boost it gives to their prestige 'back home' in their own unions.

(i) The levels of union leadership

A close examination of the power structure within the General

Council reveals that the hierarchy is complicated. There are actually four levels of power, with about half the Council on the outer or most distant edge and the other half divided among the first three levels in about equal proportions.

The top level or 'gold plated six'[3] includes those union leaders who sit on all three top TUC committees as well as (with one exception) on the National Economic Development Council (NEDC). In 1979 when Mrs Thatcher took office this group included David Basnett, Frank Chapple, Geoffrey Drain, Terry Duffy, Moss Evans and Tom Jackson.[4] Only Chapple did not sit on the NEDC but was a part of this group in every other respect.

There are a number of other members of these same committees but only this group sits on each one. Holding those positions, the six clearly have access and influence on the most important matters of policy that the TUC addresses. They are the persons who have the right and duty to represent the TUC at the highest level of consultations and bargaining with government. This does not mean that they are collectively involved in every major issue. But it does mean that they can expect to be consulted and their opinions given weight in every case.

Membership in this special inner circle is achieved in different ways. Two members of this group hold their places because they represent unions which comprise so large a share of the total TUC membership. Moss Evans and Terry Duffy speak and vote and pay for more than 3.2 million trade unionists, which is about 25 per cent of the entire TUC membership. Evans and Duffy therefore simply cannot be ignored. They carry too much weight, both within the movement itself and independently.

The other members of the group did not 'inherit' their positions. David Basnett, for example, reached the inner circle for several reasons. He does head one of the TUC's largest unions, the General and Municipal Workers Union. This did not make him an automatic candidate but it made him hard to ignore. In addition, Basnett has served a long tenure on the General Council and by its seniority system he would naturally have earned a chance to take his place at the top. Basnett also is so personally articulate and impressive as well as demanding that it would not be hard to imagine that in a totally open situation he would have risen to the top under his own steam. Of course, this logic can also be applied to Evans and Duffy, who had to display considerable talents to get to the top of their enormously large unions. So, although they inherited their places at the TUC, they had in effect 'won' their positions through considerable skill elsewhere.

Tom Jackson is another example. He has headed the Post Office Workers since he was very young and thus is one of the longest-serving members of the General Council. He has clearly gained his place in great part by his long tenure. At the same time, Jackson is such a good-natured and agreeable colleague that it was easy for his fellow members to entrust authority to him.

Taken as a whole, the group, including these four leaders, represent a considerable variety of political and industrial views. They speak for about 35 per cent of the total TUC membership. They hold a spectrum of political views from left to right. In sum, they have about as much legitimacy as would be possible in a representative elite. This is an obvious requirement in an organization so large and diverse as the TUC.

The second and third echelons of leaders are fairly easy to identify. They include those who occupy memberships on the same committees. The second group is composed of leaders who sit on at least two, while the third includes those who serve on just one. Applying these criteria to 1979, the second included eight leaders: A. W. Fisher (E + GP);[5] Joe Gormley (E + I); Clive Jenkins (E + GP); Terry Parry (E + I); George Smith (E + I); Marie Patterson (I + GP), and Alan Sapper (I + GP). The third echelon includes six leaders: A. Christopher (E); Ken Gill (E); Harry Urwin (E); F. Jarvis (I); G. Lloyd (I), and J. Slater (I).

It is also interesting to compare the average length of service. Quite predictably given the seniority system, the second group had (in 1979) served about ten years on the General Council compared to just 5 years for the third group. The first group had served only about six years, but this figure was distorted by the short tenure of the 'automatic members', Duffy and Evans.

The importance of seniority on the General Council is further confirmed by looking at other members who do *not* serve on these important committees. This group comprises half or about 20 members of the Council. The average service of these individuals in 1979 was only about 1.47 years, which is dramatically lower than their senior and more powerful colleagues. To be fair, it must be noted that two or three members of this last group had other interests which caused them to want service on other less powerful TUC committees. But the fact remains that an overwhelming number were excluded by shortness of tenure on the Council.

This stress on seniority clearly serves important interests for the TUC. It provides the predictable stability of focused leadership together with predictable change. Committee chairmen and the colleagues they serve with arrive at their positions well-imbued with the elan as well as the details of life at the trade union centre. This degree of socialization is important because work at the TUC requires information and patterns of interactions which are different from those which union leaders have acquired within their own unions. The fact that the TUC is a massive federal organization of independent unions that deals with national governments is evidence enough of this difference.

Even the most self-assured and powerful of union leaders has been amazed and even overwhelmed by the work of the TUC. Moss Evans, for one, readily admits that he was greatly surprised by what he disco ered after he joined the General Council.[7] He had always thought that the TUC was little more than a 'talking shop' of old fuddy-duddies. After three years of service, however, he was quite willing to admit to having considerable respect for the organization. Although he still jealously guards his independent power, he now believes that the TUC's work is vital and integral to the success of his own union, the Transport and General Workers. He is also now in considerably greater awe of his colleagues on the General Council and of the TUC staff. He feels that they are shrewd, well-informed and are certainly better prepared to deal with the myriad of national issues than he could ever be with only the assistance of his research department.

Seniority also tends to link up well with the TUC's main purpose which is to speak for the movement with government. The slow and long term climb that union leaders must endure in order to gain leadership roles on the General Council dovetails well with the pattern of national political change. While trade unions are much more assured than politicians that they will succeed through seniority, they meet at the highest rung political leaders who are also the products of long-term promotion. Political leaders do have a countervailing advantage that once they reach the top they tend to remain in the Cabinet or shadow Cabinet for relatively longer periods than unionists, who are bound by the rule of retirement at age 65.

The now retired leader of the Transport Workers and of the TUC, Jack Jones, is a good example. Jones won an immediate place at the top of the TUC hierarchy when he became General Secretary of his union during the late sixties. He thus gained the instant right to debate with the likes of Barbara Castle and Prime Minister Harold Wilson. However, unlike his political counterparts, he was required to give up that position at a moment of supreme power and influence, solely because he turned 65. Michael Foot, by contrast, is about the same age as Jones. But Foot has recently started his career as leader of the Labour Party with the potential of becoming the next Labour Prime Minister.

(ii) The socialization of General Council members

How members of the General Council are socialized into their roles as national union leaders is important to the TUC's behaviour as a pressure group. It is no accident that the organization is relatively conservative, cautious, reactive, defensive and consistent over the years. The comments of Moss Evans described above do much to illustrate how important socialization can be in determining the role which even the most powerful and independent of union leaders will play.

Evans and all of his colleagues on the Council reached their positions after years of struggle to gain the very top of their unions. Having reached the General Council itself, they are at the very pinacle of prestige and influence within the whole movement itself. Their paths to this lofty place have been diverse but they share demonstrated political skills. This means that they have blended in various ways personal attractiveness, a keen appreciation for the details, nuances and manipulation of substantive issues, a dose of flexibility and reasonableness as well as a patience that they would get their turn to be in the spotlight. They are, in sum, 'winners' and they interact on the Council with others who also have demonstrated that they are 'winners'.

Once on the Council these leaders confront a new union hierarchical structure which is both familiar and different from the organization within which they developed and succeeded. They start at the bottom in an exclusive club which they had long hoped to join. They want to be members because life at the top is sweet and a confirmation of who they have become, both for themselves and for their constituent members. It is heady indeed, therefore, for newly installed members of the General Council to go back to their own unions with stories of hobnobbing with the great figures of the TUC and of the government. The transcripts of annual union conferences are filled each year with copious references by General Secretaries to their incumbency on the General Council. In the same way, these leaders do not miss an opportunity to contribute similar references to stories in their union periodicals, whether supportive of TUC positions or critical of such policies. Just being on the national level with its access to important people makes service on the General Council very valuable.

This point was well illustrated during the late sixties when the TUC's policies were under intra-union attack and its prestige accordingly much weakened. The power of the shop stewards movement was increasing dramatically as shop floor wage bargaining became very important. National union leaders were logically suffering by the loss of this power and by their willingness to support the restraint of free bargaining in a government incomes policy. For the militant union member, the TUC had become a real nuisance standing in the way of an increase of their living standards – which is the essence of trade union purpose. And yet, it is striking that during this difficult period, the prestige and influence of General Council members on the national stage reached an all-time high. The attention from the press, the velocity of consultations with government both overshadowed the reality of their diminished power to control the course of policies compared to that which their predecessors had enjoyed. They became celebrities who were respected and revered for their access, if not for their opinions.

The revival of prestige and influence for General Council members during the seventies under the Wilson and Callaghan Governments thus only added to the stake that each member holds in his membership on the Council. And that stake very much includes success for the Council's work. Success has different meanings for each individual member, but there is a high degree of common purpose. Within the context of their strongly protected individuality, all want the Council and therefore the TUC to be as influential with government as possible. This goal is clearly related to their basic protective interests. They also want the Council to be authoritive in intra-union relations to the extent that it can keep the peace. This power must particularly include the influence to settle intra-union rivalries including membership recruiting arguments. Finally, they want the Council to be effective and successful in a way which relates to each of them personally. That means that the Council adopt and win influence for policies which they and their unions are particularly concerned about.

All of these purposes tend to work to foster cautious, sensitive and cooperative behaviour on the Council.[8] There are indeed, it must be stressed, moments of high tension and conflict as there was over the Isle of Grain controversy and other similar intra-union rivalries. International issues, especially as they relate to interaction with Communist-Bloc unions tend to produce ideological divisions. But these disagreements tend to be sporadic and short-lived. The more important pattern is that the Council works smoothly and deferentially. It usually goes along with the recommendations of its committees, its senior members and the General Secretary.

General Council meetings thus tend to be relatively dull and routine affairs punctuated in any given year by the occasional crisis in one of the problem areas. Senior union leaders and the General Secretary dominate the meetings. Most of the time – by some accounts 99 per cent – is taken up with committee reports which are usually accepted without wide disagreements though there is often a good deal of discussion. Newer members are usually quiet: watching, learning and waiting for the seniority system to give them their chance. They intervene actively when they see their own union interests threatened, or when their stake in Council success is at risk because of serious fissures among the membership. But in the main, they make their contributions by deferring to the highly focused leadership of the TUC's interlocking directorate – though, of course, without contributing important shares of their own authority.

2. THE GENERAL SECRETARY

The General Secretary is the TUC's leading figure.[9] He is, in effect, the chair of the interlocking directorate of union leaders and staff officials. His power includes both the formal right to speak and act in the name of the TUC, as well as the actual power to inform, coordinate and execute policy decisions in every area of the TUC's concern.

The General Secretary is undoubtedly the major legatee of the TUC's move from the fringes of power into the centre of national decision-making. As government has wanted and then needed the TUC's consultation and cooperation, it has more and more sought out the General Secretary as the key spokesperson for the trade union movement. Crisis after crisis for more than three decades has worked to focus and enhance this power even more in his hands.

The General Secretary does share authority with other members of the interlocking directorate but he is clearly first among equals. He controls the TUC organization, dominates staff relationships and coordinates the development and maintainance of rapport between members of the General Council, its committees, the staff and himself. In all this work, he seeks to maximize TUC power. It is his responsibility to take the lead in resolving at any one time as well as over time the dilemma caused by the argument over the distribution of power within the union movement.

Members of the General Council have never forgotten this responsibility when deciding whom to nominate as a new General Secretary. The Council has always held the right to choose any person it wishes for this job, but in every case has decided to appoint a TUC 'civil servant' rather than some powerful union leader.[10] The argument that so 'political' a job should be held by a union leader who has already achieved national prominence and demonstrated his skill as a bargainer with the great ministers of the day is a powerful one. But in the minds of the members of the General Council it has always been more important that the General Secretary be able to arbitrate among the conflicting and complex interests within the union movement so as to finesse as much as possible the TUC's congenital weakness.[11]

How General Secretaries have done this work while meeting the demands of collectivist politics has varied depending on their personalities, their philosophical perceptions and the circumstances they encountered. A close examination of the three General Secretaries who have served during the last two decades demonstrates the continuity and differences of their individual contribution to the TUC's effectiveness as a pressure group.

(i) Len Murray

Len Murray has been General Secretary since 1973. Like his predecessors, Murray worked his way up the staff hierarchy to the top over a period of more than a decade and a half. His first boss was George Woodcock whom he succeeded as head of the Economic Department. He then followed Woodcock's path up the ladder, becoming Assistant General Secretary under Victor Feather and then General Secretary when Feather retired. None of these promotions surprised anyone who knew Murray at the TUC, and Murray himself fully expected to be General Secretary even while he still headed the Economic Department.[12] There were occasional references by union leaders to a different succession, such as the appointment of a union leader or perhaps one of Murray's competitors at the TUC, such as Ken Graham. But no one, including Murray, ever took this chatter seriously. Murray had always been careful to keep his credibility intact and therefore didn't need to work very hard politically for the job.

What made Murray so relaxed about his succession was not just the history of staff succession as such, as much as an understanding of the dynamics of leadership at the TUC. Murray's own position as head of the Economic Department gave him just the right credentials and the chance to build an attractive reputation. Murray's own expertise as an economist was particularly important. It is, after all, about economic matters that the Government seeks out TUC advice, acquiescence and cooperation. Murray was the person who could best deliver that relationship and therefore was far more valuable in his expertise than any possible competitor, whether union leader or department head from another area within the TUC.

From an internal TUC point of view, Murray also had the advantage that he stood away from the serious fissures which always threaten the cohesion and thus the effectiveness of the TUC. Like his predecessors, he was not party to the bitter intra-union rivalries over such conflicting issues as membership recruitment which create the hard feelings and unacceptable candidacies for all-union leadership. Nor was he regarded as a participant in the ideological split between left and right.[13] Murray did make his views clear on the great economic issues of the day in his role as head of the Economic Department. But in this work, he held the advantage of speaking as an expert and not as a participant in the collective bargaining process who is subject to charges of self-interest in the way union leaders inevitably suffer. To the contrary, guiding highly charged economic policy recommendations through the Economic Committee and the General Council on hundreds of occasions sharpened his sensitivity to consensus building as it made his skills in this medium seem quite attractive and legitimate to his union leader constituents.

(a) Murray's view of TUC power

Murray is the first General Secretary of the TUC whose employment as a member of the staff dates from the postwar era. This difference helps to explain his view of the TUC's power and influence.

Murray shares considerable ground with his predecessors.[14] Like Woodcock and Feather, he is very mindful of the gains the TUC made in the postwar years. He is impressed by the contrasting image of a nearly impotent TUC during the interwar depression years with the powerful TUC after 1945, bargaining with the government on an endless agenda of issues. He is in agreement with his predecessors who were also his teachers that it was a Labour government that brought trade unionism into the management of the economy and thus firmly cemented its claim to a role in national decision-making. This development in turn produces the central thesis that the TUC is more powerful in its relationship with its constituent unions depending on how much those constituent unions fear government behaviour or love that behaviour because it gives them opportunity for gains they would not otherwise win. The TUC, in sum, is thus the natural legatee of union involvement in a collectivist process.

Murray shows how he differs from his predecessors, even the outspoken and transitional Woodcock, by his assessment of the TUC's participation in the early days of collectivist politics. Tewson and his contemporaries were quite pleased with union performance during the Attlee years.[15] They were most impressed by the *fact* of TUC participation, and also pleased by the policy rewards which their fidelity to the Labour government had produced. The TUC remained loyal to that Government including all of the elements of the managed economy and social welfare programmes. When economic crisis threatened, the TUC pitched in and accepted the Government's demands that it sacrifice by accepting a strong wage restraint even though it abhorred the policy as threatening to the well-being of its membership. But those difficult times and the sacrifices they engendered are still regarded as slight compared to the euphoria of participation.

Murray does acknowledge the importance of those times. However, he is far more critical of that leadership for their failure to recognize and defend their interests with the Labour Government.[16] Murray believes that those leaders, including the great giants of the movement – Deakin, Williamson, Geddes and others – were too enamoured with simply 'coming to the table'. They were willing to pay too high a price. They tended, he argues, to agree to just about everything the government asked for, which in turn caused a gradual schism to develop between national union leaders and their members on the shop floor. That gap between the two elements of the union movement has never been fully closed with the result that national union leaders have been undermined at crucial times during the last two decades.

This problem in turn addresses the vital questions of TUC power which so interest Murray. He is anxious that the TUC not only retain its influence in the collectivist process but that it work to optimize that influence.[17] This is a difficult and ongoing process, which segments into two challenges. The first is the task of winning and exercising power from member unions. The second is having influence with government. Both are inexorably linked.

(b) The role of circumstance and personality in Murray's leadership

Contextual and personality factors are also important in understanding the contribution of the General Secretary to the decision-making process at the TUC. Len Murray is a quiet and introspective man who makes very few splashy headlines. He is so much less flamboyant than his predecessor, Victor Feather, that he often seems the personification of the gray civil servant. However, he is a capable public spokesman in an unspectacular way. He delivers clear, concise though dry speeches and his press comments are always rational and to the point. While he does not portray the 'can do' energy of Feather, he does portray a competent and sensible image. This sort of public view has often been useful for the TUC at times such as during the 'winter of discontent'. At those moments, the union movement has appeared out-of-control, rebellious and, to some, the wreckers of British society. Murray's quiet and intelligent personality seems to portray just the right impression in those circumstances.

Inside the TUC and to his General Council colleagues, Murray is a different person. He seems much more forceful and opinionated than his bland public image.[18] He does not fit the part of the back-slapping, joke-telling conversationalist, but he does take on a softer, more human and social profile. Certainly as compared to the difficult George Woodcock, Murray comes across to his colleagues as a friendly and enjoyable personality who is well-liked. Most importantly, Murray is highly respected for his perceptiveness. In this, he is more like Woodcock than like Feather: he is again an intellectual rather than a fixer of deals, but he does not eschew 'doing the deal' in the way Woodcock did.

Murray is a strong force within the TUC staff though he has increasingly insulated himself from the hustle and bustle of its work.[19] Since his heart attack in 1976, Murray has spent much more time in his office. His leadership is exercised largely through his senior assistants, and particularly through his Assistant General Secretaries: Ken Graham, a former secretary of the Organization Department, and David Lea, former head of Economics. He has delegated to them the job of speaking and deciding in his name – though they are careful to consult with him on important matters. This has helped to keep him much freer than he was before their appointment, and certainly freer than his predecessors. He uses this extra time to concentrate on the larger issues and to maintain the necessary political relationships within the union leadership which solidify his position.

Contextually, Murray has been General Secretary of the TUC during a period of rapid and often tumultuous change. On one dimension, he has experienced the roller coaster of serious conflict with a Tory government, followed by unprecedented alliance and influence with a Labour government, followed by the chaos of the 'winter of discontent', and most recently, the bitter but restrained conflict with the Thatcher Conservative Government. On another dimension, he has experienced the incumbency of an inordinately powerful group of senior union colleagues who dominated the TUC through 1978, and from then on the succession of a group of weaker, confused and inexperienced leaders.

Looking at the dimension of union leadership during his tenure, it is important to note that Murray took office as General Secretary with a very strong team of senior union officials already in place. This group included Jack Jones, Hugh Scanlon, Lord Greene, Lord Allen and David Basnett. Jones was especially influential and became even more so during the Wilson and Callaghan Governments. During this period, Murray operated more as a broker and mediator than dynamic leader in his own right. He clearly acquiesced to Jones and the others, particularly in the deference he gave them to speak and represent the TUC publicly. In private, he was more dynamic, particularly before his 1976 heart attack. His efforts were directed at maximizing the strength of the TUC position with the Labour Government and in this work he was especially effective at opening and preserving access to ministers. He particularly nurtured the Jack Jones – Michael Foot relationship which proved to be so fruitful.

Later, in 1978, when Jones, Scanlon and most of the others had retired or were about to retire, Murray took up a more aggressive role. He became much more public and dominated the new and weaker group of union leaders.[20] By then, the situation they faced was much more frustrating and fraught with danger for the TUC's position at the centre of national decision-making. Growing unemployment, low productivity, falling industrial production, tight monetary policy and especially unprecedentedly high postwar unemployment sapped union power. The growing unwillingness of Labour ministers to 'pony up' rewards for further union economic cooperation also undermined the social contract and created serious tensions.

Murray found his job increasingly difficult and frustrating in these circumstances. There seemed to be no rallying point on which to project his leadership. He was articulate in denouncing Labour's policies and then later Mrs Thatcher's policies, but he was unable to produce a credible or attractive counterforce or argument. Without such a rallying point, he and his colleagues seemed confused and hesitant. The image of weakness which they portrayed was made even more telling by memories of their seemingly bold and successful predecessors.

The other dimension of Murray's stewardship at the TUC has been the differences and changes in party government. Murray took office in the midst of the growing controversy between the miners and Prime Minister Heath. He was thus thrown instantly into a politically charged crisis. The course of that dispute leading to Mr Heath's defeat in the February 1974 election produced an image of Murray as a partisan General Secretary. This impression has stuck.

For Conservatives, Murray has seemed to be the most political and anti-Tory General Secretary in history. Former Prime Minister Heath, for one, has repeatedly blamed Murray for partisan scheming during the miners' conflict.[22] For Heath, Murray is the bad opposite of Victor Feather whom he believes was a good and responsible General Secretary. Heath confidently speculates that if Feather had continued in office he would have negotiated a peaceful end to the 1973–4 crisis.

Heath obviously holds a self-interest grudge in this matter. But he is not alone in his views. Tory colleagues share his suspicions about Murray to the point that they have constructed a kind of mythology about him and the TUC staff. Mrs Thatcher's own anti-collectivist views are partially rooted in her own perceptions of the 1973–4 débâcle. Although she was a legatee of Mr Heath's defeat, she is not about to suffer her rival's mistake. For her as well as her confidants, Mr Heath made the mistake of thinking he could negotiate and even bargain with the union movement. She believes that this sort of collectivism is both a mistake in the exercise of democratic government as well as a fatal trap for any responsible politician.

In truth, Murray's view of the Tories is less inflammatory than their impression of him. He is by nature more distant, aloof and less inclined to have the heart-to-heart chats over drinks that Feather enjoyed. Feather seemed to make it a personal challenge to gain the confidence of the Tory leadership and he was quite proud of the access and rapport he developed with Heath, even in the most adverse circumstances. Murray, by contrast, does not relish this kind of effort and tends to be more pointed about his relationship with Tories and their government. He has frequently pointed out that he is naturally less likely to agree with Conservatives in power than with Labour.[23] But he is equally assertive that he thinks it important that the TUC have relations with Tories. As he said at the beginning of his time as General Secretary, in 1973, 'We may not agree with them but at least we ought to know about them and so this is something that happens from time to time'.[24] His is therefore the traditional TUC view of Tory government and mirrors the statement the General Council adopted when Churchill led the Conservatives back into office in 1951. In more diplomatic terms, it would be fair to describe Murray's purpose in dealing with the Tories as building a relationship which is 'cool but correct'.

Murray's relations with the Labour Party are quite different though no less complex. He was openly delighted when the Wilson Government replaced the Conservatives at the beginning of 1974. He had frequently insisted that the union movement holds natural ties to the Labour Party. These ties make it quite logical that the TUC will agree more often with Labour politicians and enjoy a better access and influence leading to its views being taken into account when policy is made. This was especially true in 1974 when Labour took office sensitized both to the reasons for Heath's defeat and to the 'social contract' which the two sides of the Labour movement had agreed during the years of opposition.

Murray also makes no secret about his affection for the Labour Party in personal terms. But his sentiments as well as his delight at Labour's return to office in 1974 must be viewed through the lens of conscious union self-interest. Murray is first and foremost the General Secretary of the TUC. His support for the Labour Party cannot therefore exceed the distance the Party travels to protect and enhance union purpose. To go beyond this interest in bestowing his loyalty on the party would be to create just the sort of dangerous situation which he feels that older unionists created when they paid too high a price for their inclusion in the decision-making process. This approach, he believes, produced the destabilizing schism between the shop floor and the national union movement, with the ultimate result that it weakened the power of the TUC.

The actual course of the Labour Government from 1974 until 1979 did, in fact, produce just such a dilemma for Murray. It sorely tested his political fidelity and created serious tensions and conflicts within the ruling directorate at Congress House. The 'winter of discontent' produced a crisis in the relationship which is not yet resolved.

(ii) George Woodcock

In philosophical terms, Len Murray is the disciple of George Woodcock, the TUC's great exponent of trade union participation in collectivism. No General Secretary, save Lord Citrine, dominated the TUC by the force of his ideas and personality as Woodcock did for the decade from 1960.

Woodcock's career at the TUC followed a pattern which was almost identical to that of Len Murray. He was an Assistant in the Economic Department and then its Secretary. He was chosen ahead of Victor Feather to be Assistant General Secretary and then succeeded Tewson as General Secretary more or less automatically.

Woodcock was an extremely bright and perceptive person. So many writers have made this comment about Woodcock that the remark is almost a cliche. But his brilliance, demonstrated early in life by his first class honours at Oxford, must be recognized in order to understand his role at the TUC. For Woodcock was a real intellectual in the midst of colleagues who were not only of a very different temperament but who disliked intellectuals.[25] Woodcock recognized this contradiction and returned it in his own dislike for the rough and tumble bargaining milieu which his trade union leader colleagues embraced and of which they were superb practitioners.

The relationship between himself and 'them' was thus predictably uncomfortable. He was impossibly overbearing to most of the General Council.[26] He never displayed his differences with them gently. He bellowed his views and demanded acquiescence. He also rejected personal politics, doing nothing more to win support for his views than to let his own be heard. He refused to socialize, enjoying his distance and aloofness. He was not to be part of the 'dirty, shabby, deal'. He would have it his way by the sheer force of his intellect or he would not have it at all.

Woodcock's personality mixed with the agenda of TUC business to produce an imbalanced pattern of leadership. Woodcock took powerful and dominating control of those areas and issues which he found interesting. But he neglected and in effect abdicated nearly all leadership in a great many other areas of TUC concern which he found 'boring'. Economics, of course, was his first love, and there was not one on the General Council who could or would challenge his authority in that area.[27] Whereas he was often sullen and uncommunicative about most TUC business as it came before the General Council, he would turn passionate and articulate about economic policy. Victor

Feather, for one, never ceased to be amazed how Woodcock could wallow so long in uncommunicative 'grunts' and then explode into powerful, articulate and persuasive prose.[28] At his best, he was spellbinding. He would lecture his colleagues like an authoritarian parent his children. These episodes did not leave room for debate or questions. His ideas were delivered as the gospel and Woodcock was so powerful that they were taken as such by his usually intimidated audience. Members of the General Council grumbled out loud about Woodcock's personality and his overbearing approach, but they usually took his advice and gave him their respect.[29] When he left the TUC to head the Commission on Industrial Relations in 1969, just short of retirement anyway, there was widespread pleasure that he was gone. However, there was also widespread fear of the intellectual vacuum he had left behind. Many of the senior union leaders demonstrated how important Woodcock really was to them by the frequent efforts they made to get his advice in his retirement.[30]

(a) Woodcock's view of TUC power

But what of his views? What was his purpose? Woodcock was an activist in the robes of a preachy philosopher. His image of the Trades Union Congress was of a powerful, centralized spokesgroup working actively for the interests of the trade union movement at all times and in all circumstances.[31] He came to power and in fact rose to power primarily during the years when the TUC was drawn into the centre of national decision-making. He also saw and participated in the relationship between the TUC and Labour's first majority government. Woodcock endorsed, in fact wholeheartedly embraced, this development. But unlike Tewson or the colleagues of his time as General Secretary like Deacon and Lawther, Woodcock was not in awe of trade union's new position. He was not worried that it would disappear if trade unionism was too demanding of the relationship. Rather, he was afraid that unionism would demand too little of itself and be willing to give too little to exploit its influence.

Woodcock's views flowed from two theses.[32] First, he accepted the legitimacy of the collectivist process. Trade unionism, he believed, was at the centre of power because government had needed to draw it there. In doing so, British political leaders were responding to the demands made upon them by the electorate that government manage the economy in order to produce what they hoped would be a permanent state of well-being. Woodcock believed that this commitment to manage the economy was so powerful that it could not be reversed. For trade unionism, the commitment was an important opportunity that could not be avoided. The TUC, for its part, was in a position both to promote policies which it wanted and to protect the movement as well as individual unions from policies which were negative. Whatever the level of opportunity though, Woodcock also believed that trade unionism had no choice but to participate in collectivism. To do otherwise was to invite the government-of-the-day to take actions which would compel that participation on an unfavourable basis.

Woodcock's other thesis was that trade unionism was ill-suited to meet the opportunity and therefore was at considerable risk. The problem as he saw it was that the trade union movement is a very large democratic federation suffering from inevitable diversity and size. Trade unions leaders are activists only in a wages sense. Otherwise, they are a highly conservative group. Many of them are progressives as individuals, but by experience have become cautious. The TUC finds it difficult simply to make decisions and often finds it impossible to make controversial decisions. Most of the leadership wants to take the least aggressive position in order to keep change at a minimum and their individual union power at a maximum. Even more pessimistically, though, Woodcock frequently complained that once the trade union centre did decide to 'pull the lever' of decision-making, nothing happened; or if it did happen, it would happen with seriously diminishing effect as the decision rippled out to the union movement at large.[33]

But how to get his colleagues even to 'pull the lever' at all? Woodcock believed that his major task as General Secretary was to convince, cajole and otherwise prod the General Council to make decisions that reached above the lowest common denominator. He sought to develop a more dynamic trade unionism in order to take advantage of the opportunity it had at being at the centre of national decision-making.

From this point of view, government was his greatest ally.[34] Government needed union attention to its policy requirements. Woodcock felt that he could use this pressure to force change. He hoped government would stir the union movement to reform itself so as to maximize the opportunity its place at the centre of power provided. This meant that the TUC would become successful at convincing government to favour positive union interests while being influential in rejecting policies which potentially undermined its interests. At the same time, Woodcock was keenly aware of the inevitable impatience that government leaders would bring to bear in this process. He recognized that while the TUC in particular would want to use government pressure to galvanize union activity, the TUC would also want to find a way to deflect inordinate pressure for cooperation which if unsatisfied might cause the political system to restrict voluntary trade union behaviour.

Both of these theories help to explain Woodcock's policy views: why he championed structural reform at the TUC and why he was in favour of economic planning, of incomes policy and militantly against government efforts to legislate restraint on union behaviour in the form of industrial relations legislation. At heart, Woodcock was a nationalist in the trade union movement. He was unconcerned about party ties; instead, he focused almost entirely on winning the purposes and goals of trade unionism. He could work with any government in that pursuit, using the advantage of the managed economy while working to fend off political impatience. He was thus different from his predecessor, Vincent Tewson, who delighted in just being 'part of the action' and in gratitude was always eager to take what government – especially Labour government – might offer. Woodcock better fitted the generation of new trade unionists who no longer worried about the possiblity of the man around the corner waiting for his job. Rather, he saw full employment as the keystone of modern trade union power. Unions would have to pay a certain price for their power by restraining their wage demands in order to preserve and foster a growing economy, but in other ways they could – for the first time in history – make real gains in the standard of living of their members. The opportunity for real gain was there, in his view, and the trade union movement should not let its own weakness and timidity stand in the way of getting it.

(b) Woodcock's conduct in office

George Woodcock's actual experience as General Secretary for nine years was much less rewarding than his brilliant credentials had promised. It was mostly an exercise in frustration for him, buffered partially by the satisfaction he felt at being in such firm control of the TUC. The very elements of his personality and style which gave him such command also worked to undermine the possibility that his ideas would win practical implementation with either his union colleagues or with political leaders.

His greatest weakness was his rejection of practical politics.[35] He steadfastly refused to become involved with those 'shabby deals' which are so central to any political process. On the one hand, Woodcock would promote the notion of working with government in order to influence policy-making, yet on the other hand he would not exert himself to politic for his views with his colleagues or with ministers. Long discussions and arguments about the merits of the issue were legitimate tactics, but he would do no arm-twisting, no deals and no socializing which might have otherwise smoothed the way.

Wage politics was the key issue of Woodcock's time and best illustrates his leadership. Wage restraint had by Woodcock's tenure in office become an important point of conflict within the union movement and with the government-of-the-day. The prevailing view among politicians as well as trade union leaders and leading economists – and George Woodcock – was that wage inflation was the natural outcome of government sponsored and maintained full employment. It was an inevitable 'side effect' of the commitment of 1944 to provide the citizens of Britain with a better and more secure life in the postwar era. As such, from the earliest days, there was widespread recognition among elites that some way would have to be found to restrain the inflationary pressure of full employment if it was not to be the tragic instrument by which Britain lost vital price competitiveness for its products in the world markets.

George Woodcock agreed fully with this thinking. As a trade union leader, he was especially concerned that the wage restraint issue not become the sledgehammer which a desperate government might use to destroy the new influence trade unionism enjoyed.[36] His view was that trade unionism, with the TUC holding a leading role, should recognize not only the government's interests in this matter but the independently sensible notion that restraint simply must be exercised in order to protect the viability of the many goals attendant on government's management of the economy. He felt that the TUC should take the lead in working out a policy of wage restraint based on voluntary compliance. By keeping the terms and policing of restraint in union hands, Woodcock felt that the chances for compliance would be enhanced significantly. More importantly, he felt it important to forestall any tendency on the part of government to usurp union power or in any way interfere with the functioning of the free collective bargaining process.

The coming to power of a Labour Government in 1964 gave particular currency to the tension between government and unions. Whereas the Tories were always intimidated by the combination of their memories of the 1926 General Strike and their lack of closeness to individual union leaders, the Labour Government enjoyed just the opposite relationship. It was an activist administration dedicated to a more aggressive management of the economy. Moreover, its leaders were brethren of the movement, part of the family. They expected and indeed insisted that their colleagues on the union side of the labour movement contribute to the success of 'their' government by cooperating in the policies which the political leaders would enunciate. While George Woodcock himself was little impressed with these calls to familial loyalty, he knew his General Council would be. And more importantly, he knew that unless the Government got what it wanted from the unions it would not wait long to make its policies compulsory – something a Conservative government would have been far more wary to do at that time.

Thus, as Woodcock viewed his job in late 1964 and 1965, the new Labour Government needed to be convinced to make good on its promise to promote economic growth and develop a long-term and slowly evolving *voluntary* incomes policy.[37] The General Council, at the same time, needed to learn to accept the inevitability of voluntary incomes policy while remembering to stress union interests in assessing the inevitable demand by the new Government for acquiescence to its leadership in every area of policy-making.

It was a difficult task, requiring political dexterity and argumentative skills. Woodcock was certainly equipped with the argumentative skills but he was in trouble from the beginning on the political side. The two foci of his efforts were the Minister for Economic Affairs and Deputy Prime Minister George Brown (now Lord George-Brown) on one hand and the General Council on the other.

(c) Woodcock vs. George Brown

George Brown had been an active trade union leader himself before he entered politics, eventually rising to compete for leadership with Harold Wilson after Gaitskell died. Brown, widely known as being on the right of the Labour Party, was also well known for his cynicism about his old colleagues in the union movement.[38] He openly espoused the theory that a slothful, greedy union movement had contributed much to Britain's economic problems and recurring crises. However, it was Brown's job in the new government to head a new Department of Economic Affairs and therefore to promote economic growth. Though he found only enthusiasm from the TUC about his marching orders, he found only disagreement about his views. For Brown believed that one of his urgent tasks was to goad the union movement into a more progressive and cooperative stance; to create a kind of economic partnership with the government.

George Woodcock not only didn't agree with Brown about how to get the union movement 'moving', he didn't have much use for him personally.[39] Brown is a plain spoken, ebullient personality who was a study in contrast to Woodcock's intellectual aloofness. Brown tended to want to do things 'now' and in his way. Woodcock was no less insistent about his views but certainly more evolutionary and voluntary in his projection of union–government relations. Most importantly, Brown was a politician in every sense, being far more interested in the negotiations of deals than the substance of issues, both of which Woodcock abhorred. It was perhaps inevitable therefore that the two men would clash heatedly over so sensitive an issue as wage policy.

Ironically, both started from a common agreement that wage restraint was inevitable. When Brown told Woodcock within a few days of taking office that the Government wanted an incomes policy, Woodcock said that he was in full agreement.[40] The difference between them was about how to proceed and what could be expected, not about the purpose. This commonality between the two might have been effective but it proved much less so as discussions continued. For Brown the politician was prepared from the beginning of the relationship to use his political talents to outflank the apolitical General Secretary.

Woodcock soon found that his position with Brown was sub-

stantially weakened by Brown's aggressive use of his long-
standing personal relationships with a number of members of the
General Council. Taking this approach, Brown made it a regular
habit to take any issue about which he disagreed with Woodcock
directly to the members of the General Council privately and
individually.[41] The result was that Brown kept Woodcock off
balance and ultimately pressed the General Council successfully
to adopt positions which irritated its own General Secretary.

What was particularly interesting about Brown's successful
challenge of Woodcock in this way was that he convinced the
General Council to 'go along' with positions which were increasingly seen as collaborationist by shop floor leaders within the
union movement. The majority on the General Council was still
tilted in that direction at this time, but not nearly so much so as
had been the case during the forties and fifties. Already the more
militant shop stewards movement was insisting that the national
leadership act more aggressively to protect union interests as
compared to party interests. Woodcock, in these matters, sided
with the militants but for reasons which were slightly different.

The crux of the dispute, which tended to reoccur between
himself and Brown, was over the timing and development of
incomes policy.[42] Woodcock kept insisting on long-term
development as the only way to have real incomes policy. Brown
kept insisting on immediate targets and other assurances needed
by the government to assuage international financiers who were
engaged in a disastrous run on the pound. Thus Woodcock did
not so much side with the pure militants in rejecting wage
restraint, as he did on rejecting the kind of restraint which Brown
wanted to thrust at the TUC for immediate implementation.

Turning to the General Council itself, Woodcock found himself
without a fund of good will, good feeling and close personal
leverage which he surely needed in embarking on so important a
series of negotiations. George Brown was a real problem because
Woodcock knew Brown would undermine his own authority.
Moreover, Woodcock could offer little defense against Brown so
long as he continued to undertake his own political counter
offensive. He had only one real ally on the General Council,
Frank Cousins, the fiery leader of the Transport Workers Union,
but Cousins had taken leave to join the Government and, at any
rate, was an arch foe of wage restraint policy. Thus, there was
really   no   one   that   Woodcock   could   count

on to show loyalty to him and therefore to go beyond deference to the force of his arguments or the authority of his position.

The details of what turned out to be about a year of negotiations leading to several wage restraint understanding between the TUC and the Government are described elsewhere.[43] Suffice for our purposes here that George Woodcock took the lead as spokesman throughout the process. He was never challenged in that role. He took the General Council's position at union conferences as well as with the media which followed each step with great interest. It would also be fair to say that Woodcock had a great impact on the directions and terms of these agreements. But it is equally important to point out that he lost several arguments with his colleagues which were important, especially as they related to his own strongly held views.

George Brown successfully out-maneuvered him in getting the General Council to accept a specific wage norm of 3½ per cent in April 1965. This despite Woodcock's very strong warning that this norm could not be held, if at all, for more than a few weeks at best. Moreover, he warned that the government would use the failure of that norm as an excuse for taking additional actions – a point which often had stirred the fears of General Council members in the past.

Five months later in the midst of another economic crisis, Brown pressed for TUC acceptance of an 'early warning' system under which unions would be required to give the government advance notice of their intention to make pay claims. Woodcock responded even more vehemently against this proposal, both in making his case to the General Council and to Brown himself. He was especially disturbed by the course of events. The Government was already showing itself to be captured by the demands of international financiers that it abandon long-term economic growth policies in favour of short-term remedies for the balance of payments deficit. The idea of an immediate wage norm in the spring was tied to this approach and, as Woodcock had warned, it was not working well enough or quickly enough to give much help to the Government. As he had feared, the Government, now impatient, was coming back for an early warning system. Acquiescence to such a scheme coming on top of the earlier events would, Woodcock felt, only weaken the credibility of union leaders and ultimately give vent to militancy on the shop floor with attendant industrial disruption. The whole scenario, moreover, would weaken the relationship between the unions and the new government. And what was worse, it would destroy the chances for the development of real incomes policy over time.

Woodcock's argument was painfully appealing to his colleagues. But George Brown's appeal for support for 'their' Government was still simply too strong. They recognized the growing problem of shop floor power as a challenge to their own authority, but they were willing to see their salvation in the success of the Labour Government which needed their help at the moment. So they rejected Woodcock and acquiesced, and the split over incomes policy and industrial relations with the' Government was put off for some months longer.

(d) Conclusion

George Woodcock is thus a powerful, important and yet somewhat sad figure in the history of Trades Union Congress. For this analysis of the role of the General Secretary, though, Woodcock is a vital figure. No General Secretary except Walter Citrine had such impact by the force of his ideas.

He was the key figure at the TUC, even as Assistant General Secretary, who best understood the significance of the economic contract of 1944. He saw the opportunities, the responsibilities as well as the threat in the union movement's new place at the centre of national economic decision-making. There is little doubt that his powerful command of the TUC propelled the movement into a real bargaining relationship with government. Yet, at the same time it is also clear that his lack of personal and political willingness forestalled the kind of success which the TUC might otherwise have achieved.

He left behind him important leaders like Len Murray, who was his student. He also left a clearer sense of union purpose as well as a more powerful role for the General Secretary. He did not achieve the redistribution of union power or his reforms of union structure which would have made the TUC more powerful and effective. He also did not achieve the cooperation and the real bargaining relationship which might have cemented the union movement's place as an effective producer group. Quite sadly, Woodcock left behind a confused union movement which had found no way to participate in rewarding collectivist politics. He also left behind a bi-partisan political will to find strategies to avoid the whole collectivist process.

(iii) Victor Feather

Victor Feather, who followed George Woodcock as General Secretary from 1969 to 1973, was a remarkable contrast. It is hard to imagine that two persons could be any more different from each other. Feather was a lively, ebullient man with nearly unlimited energy to give to his work at Congress House. He was innately optimistic compared to George Woodcock who was persistently cynical. It is not surprising then that the two men disliked each other.[44] They spent long years in rivalry and for most of that time in the difficult position of chief and his assistant chief. Woodcock was four years older than Feather and by seniority as much as any reason became the Assistant General Secretary to Tewson when Feather became Deputy Assistant Secretary. This relationship lasted for more than a dozen years. Then, for nine years, Feather served as Assistant General Secretary to Woodcock, waiting not so patiently (though loyally) for his own chance to be General Secretary. Since there is strict adherence to age-65 retirement, Feather always knew that his tenure as General Secretary would be limited to just four years.

Woodcock was an intellectual, a philosopher; Feather was a doer, a fixer, a compromiser and a wheeler-dealer. He did not so much care for theorizing as he did for smoke-filled rooms and the camaraderie of tough negotiating with friends and with adversaries alike. These were the things that electrified him. They complemented Woodcock almost perfectly and Woodcock, though he disliked Feather, relied on him at the most difficult moments to do the kind of 'dirty job' which Woodcock had absolutely no taste for.[45] Feather, after all, had come up the TUC ladder through the Organization Department while Woodcock was at the Economic. Feather therefore knew the organization and the people. He liked to deal with the constituency unions. Woodcock clearly did not. So it was his job to handle the questions of amalgamation, union organization, inter-union disputes and the growing problem of industrial strife during the sixties. As it turned out, nothing could have been better preparation for his time as General Secretary.

Feather became Acting General Secretary on March 1, 1969, when George Woodcock resigned to become Chairman of the newly created Commission on Industrial Relations (CIR). It was a difficult time. The argument about Barbara Castle's plan to legislate a new pattern of industrial relations was provoking the most serious crisis in history between the trade union movement and its partner on the political side of the labour movement. It was no time for learning on the job, for reflection or for doing much of anything other than facing this threat head-on. It proved to be the hallmark of Feather's years at the top of the TUC.

Eric Silver has written the definitive biography of Victor Feather[46]. He describes Feather as having taken the top job at the TUC on a 'negative'. But from the TUC's perspective, Feather himself was a very positive figure to emerge at just that moment. For the events of 1969 were the result of years of growing frustrations by both major political parties at their failure to win the sort of union cooperation which they perceived as necessary for the successful management of economic policy. Woodcock had been prescient when he worried out loud that government would too easily grow impatient with the slow and unpredictable reaction of the union movement to demands for effective wage restraint. Though it was industrial militancy that finally led the Wilson Government to take up legislation, it was the failure of wage restraint which really provoked the confrontation. And it was a Labour government which felt it could take the risk of forcing a showdown by attempting to legislate 'good' industrial relations.

The moment clearly demanded political skills, the kind of bargaining acumen which a Feather and not a Woodcock had. Woodcock had taken the job at the CIR as much because he was about to retire from the TUC as for any other reason, but there were also hints that he was not at all happy about leading the battle against the government. He felt particularly fatalistic about the unfolding events.[47] He felt frustrated at the failure of the Wilson Government to learn about voluntary trade unionism and to experience the patience which he had tried to teach them during the previous eight years. Now he saw nothing but disaster ahead with little of the hope for effective producer group politics which he had exuded when he took office at the beginning of the sixties.

Feather's natural optimism plus his personal skills and sense of loyalty to the unity of the labour movement were particularly appropriate to the challenge he found. The task from the beginning was to find some way for the TUC to deflect the

Government from its purpose of legislating. At the same time he strove to retain the Labour Party's integrity as a viable and electable political leadership.

Importantly, Feather's philosophical view of trade unionism and the work of the TUC was not much different from that of Woodcock's.[48] He, like Woodcock, wanted an independent TUC to be at the centre of power and influence, which meant being involved in a permanent relationship with government. The whole development of collectivist politics had covered his period at the TUC and he had been a part of it. Like Woodcock he saw the 'In Place of Strife' legislation as a direct threat to this whole era, and thus to TUC power.

Feather thus plunged into the 'In Place of Strife' struggle with all of his strategic and tactical skills. Using every means and insight he had, he gradually forced Wilson and Castle to recognize that the outcome of legislation would be the alienation of trade unionism and fracture of the Labour Party without any real chance of winning the industrial discipline they so urgently sought.[49] The TUC's victory was very much his victory. His achievements included organizing General Council solidarity and staff dedication as well as knowing how to encourage Labour MPs to play their decisive role as opponents of their own government. The alliance with Labour was saved even though the bitter consequence was undoubtedly the defeat of the Wilson Government in the general election almost exactly one year later.

As a consequence, Feather found himself back in a new battle with the comparative strangers who made up the Heath Government. In many ways it was much easier for Feather to fight Tories. It was so much easier to rally strong support against natural enemies who explicitly wanted to legislate involuntary industrial relations. Again, it was Feather's organization and personal skills which made so much difference. He skilfully developed trade union opposition while encouraging Heath to come around and face the necessity of doing business with the unions.

Feather's only real failure during this period was his inability to convert effective opposition to the Tory Government into the kind of agreement on union participation in economic decision-making which Feather himself very much wanted to achieve. Certainly one of his most successful coups in this direction was the confidence that Heath developed in Feather.[50] Heath became sincerely impressed with Feather as an insightful and reasonable leader. While Heath continued to hold a cynical view of most of Feather's colleagues on the General Council, he did feel he could work with Feather. Moreover, he went so far as to believe that this was a unique opportunity for a Conservative Prime Minister to establish real access to the trade union movement. Feather cultivated this confidence, hoping both to convince the Prime Minister to abandon his earlier harsh approach to unionism and to create the climate for union access in the other direction. Feather was so skilful in fact that he probably did some unintended disservice to his successor Len Murray, who appeared to Heath to be much more unreasonable and untrustworthy. Feather was the only one Heath trusted, so that once he retired Heath retreated from dealing with the unions or trusting their word in fear that the succeeding leadership had malicious political motives – a miscalculation which was to cost Heath his office and eventually his leadership of the Conservative Party.

This sort of highly personal politics is obviously important in a collectivist era when the arguments over policy are so loaded with economic and political import. Feather's ability to win the confidence of Heath between 1972 and 1973 was virtually unique in the long relationship between trade unionists and Conservative politicians. Only the TUC's relationship with Churchill and his Minister of Labour, Walter Monckton, was closer and more effective. The problem in the Heath period, by contrast, was that Feather was operating in a highly negative atmosphere as the only positive ray of light. He offered not just cooperation but the possibility of salvation from disaster for Heath. Heath ultimately placed too much hope in Feather and showed his misunderstanding of national trade unionism.

Feather's power at the TUC rested almost entirely on his ability to find compromise where none seemed possible. He gave the TUC coherence when it needed coherence and strength when it otherwise might have been bogged down in useless squabbling. He did not provide powerful or significant ideas. He deferred especially to the legacy of Woodcock and the contemporary ideas of Jack Jones in this regard. Feather was a politician who knew the cues of trade union politics well enough to be able to translate the otherwise constant bickering sufficiently into a decisive, albeit negative, phalanx against government policy. This was a considerable achievement. But Feather did not succeed in fashioning the sort of positive role that Woodcock had envisioned but which also eluded him.

3. THE TUC CIVIL SERVICE

It falls to the TUC civil service and particularly to the key Department Secretaries and Assistant General Secretaries to provide the 'glue' which coalesces the ruling directorate.[51] The union leaders hold the formal decision-making power and the General Secretary is clearly the TUC's leading figure, but it is the senior staff which does the hard substantive and political work leading to decision-making and policy implementation at Congress House. This work does not overcome the TUC's inherent weakness stemming from the argument over the distribution of power within the union movement. Rather, it helps the TUC 'finesse' that obstruction which gives the union movement what sense of purpose and effectiveness it has.

The key linkage person in the TUC staff decision-making and implementation process is the Department Secretary. The Secretary dispenses, receives and interprets the work of his Assistants who deal with the specific issues and projects which make up the work of the TUC. He is the liaison with the related committees of union leaders as well as up through the TUC organization to the Assistant General Secretaries and the General Secretary. No other person is better informed or in control of his area of substantive responsibility. Also it is the Department Secretary who deals on a day-to-day basis with the civil servants and government ministers. Ultimately, what the General Council hears and decides in most instances is the product of work within the Department Secretary's control.

The work of the Department Secretaries in the key areas of international and economic as well as organizational affairs is highly political, in an intra-TUC sense. The subject matters are so important that they inevitably attract an inordinate amount of attention, both public and by participating union leaders. Economic affairs especially are prone to serious crises in what has become an almost recurring cycle. This means that the Economic Secretary, for example, needs to exercise good political skills in dealing with his galaxy of 'clients'.[52]

The primary client is, of course, the committee he serves and in which his title of Secretary is rooted. He is in office for the formal purpose of serving the committee in any way that it so insists. Demands for information, recommendations or just about anything else including personal favours come from any member, though in practice the largest number of contacts a Secretary has are with the Chairman.

Serving the committee is extremely demanding and above all a political challenge. The successful Secretary inevitably relishes the task. If he has learned nothing else in his time at the TUC, he has learned how to relate to 'his committee'. His purpose is clear and consistent: he works to keep his 'lead', that is, to win from the committee sufficient confidence and trust such that he earns a large fund of discretionary power and sufficient influence to control the direction which the committee takes.[53]

(i) The Economic Department

The Economic Department is a good example.[54] Its present Secretary, Bill Callaghan, came to the Department about ten years ago when he was just out of university. He was hired as an Assistant by David Lea who was then Economic Secretary himself. His lineage therefore is very much that of George Woodcock and Len Murray. Callaghan, like those distinguished predecessors is bright, energetic, incisive and a very articulate individual. He could well have succeeded in any enterprise at considerably more pay. But he is committed to trade unionism and to the TUC specifically. He has found the TUC a good opportunity and in such a relatively small organization has enjoyed the kind of high level access and advancement as well as policy impact which he might have not had as so young a leader elsewhere. Moreover, he took up his opportunities aggressively and as a result rose rapidly within the Department. He was quickly promoted to be second in command, as Assistant Secretary. When David Lea was promoted by his mentor, Len Murray, in 1977 to be Assistant General Secretary charged with economic policy, Callaghan was in a perfect position to be promoted almost automatically to his present job (at time of writing).

Callaghan is like his fellow Department Secretaries at the TUC in that he keeps a frenzied pace. The organization is so small that interpersonal decision-making takes up a great deal of time.

Callaghan has almost no time for desk work during normal business hours. During the day, he is constantly in consultation 'upstairs', with union leaders, David Lea, government ministers or Len Murray himself. He also spends a significant amount of his time giving background interviews to journalists and scholars who are constantly researching the TUC. After hours, he reads the work of his Assistants, answers his correspondence and prepares his own reports. He usually does not arrive home before 9 p.m., which leaves very little time before he needs to head back to the office.

Throughout this hectic schedule, Callaghan keeps a firm sense of what is important. The myriad of interpersonal relationships most strongly colours the nature and success of his and his Department's work. He works hard to build and maintain a good working relationship with his Chairman. This purpose has different requirements depending on the personality of the chairman. Thus, when Lord Allen headed the Economic Committee during the middle and late seventies, Callaghan recognized and responded to Allen's inclination to allow the Department to define the Committee's work. With David Basnett now in the same role, Callaghan recognizes a quite different situation. Basnett is a more independent and demanding personality. He also has a stronger sense of his agenda. Callaghan therefore is careful to balance a deference to Basnett's leadership with his own departmental leadership. He provides excellent staff support and advice, which builds trust and confidence with Basnett, while at the same time maintaining the department's 'lead' on a wide range of business.

Though Callaghan gives an important share of his 'committee time' to this relationship, he also pays important attention to every other member of his committee. He is keenly aware that all of the members hold equal voting power and especially that several of the members such as Moss Evans and Terry Duffy are every bit as powerful as Basnett in their own right. Moreover, he knows that the pattern of succession at the TUC will produce the next chairman from among the group that he now serves.

The goal in all this effort by Callaghan is to create and maintain an effective decision-making process. This is obviously a tricky and subjective challenge in a group of individual union members who remember at every moment that they are *both* national union leaders with a common responsibility and union leaders who owe their authority to their constituent membership. They do not want to be seen, for example, to be too actively fostering incomes policy if their own unions are militantly against that policy. In such a situation, Callaghan as Secretary can provide key leadership. For instance, he can fashion a formula by which an individual leader can cooperate within the Committee to agree on a common incomes policy position without having to declare his support in public.

Callaghan's work in this kind of situation, which does occur quite often within the Committee, is very much like that which is common to legislative politics. There is an inevitable difference between the public position which leaders take and their behaviour within more private decision-making bodies. Consensual, democratic politics simply requires a delicate give and take. It is not well served by dogmatic, inflexible views even though the process of bidding for wide support encourages just such clear, simple and appealing positions. Of course, the TUC has severe problems in this way. Callaghan thus serves as the facilitator, the 'fixer' who looks for and then tries to build support for a common position between competing views, ideologies and political imperatives. It is in this way that the TUC, in all of its areas of work, reaches decisions which are as much above the 'lowest common denominator' as possible.

This committee process is so pivotal at the TUC because what the General Council addresses is primarily what its committees report. Moreover, the Council usually approves its recommendations without substantial changes. This means that the work that Bill Callaghan and his colleagues in other departments accomplish usually becomes TUC policy. Once such policy is formally approved by the General Council, it usually reverts to officials like Callaghan to be implemented.

This description is not meant to create the impression that the Department Secretary operates completely with his own authority and in isolation. He is the central figure in a complex process, and he *is* subordinate and responsible not just to union leaders but to the Assistant General Secretaries and up through to Len Murray. He is constantly offering and testing his ideas and leadership with those above him.

Callaghan, in particular, is in constant touch with David Lea about the work of his committee. In many ways the relationship is similar to what it was when Lea himself headed the department.

This interlocking relationship does add considerable authority to the work of the Economic Department which does make an important difference during crucial bargaining. Lea simply has more power, as does Callaghan in turn, to settle issues in the name of the General Secretary and, in many senses, for the General Council as well.

Further up the line, Lea and Callaghan do consult with Len Murray. George Woodcock took a direct hand in economic policy-making throughout his term as General Secretary. Len Murray, by contrast, has surprised some of his colleagues by taking a more indirect approach. He has allowed Lea to take the role Woodcock did, while reserving his own involvement for the most important and dramatic issues. This relationship expresses quite well the trust which Murray places in Lea and in turn in Callaghan. It also demonstrates the consequences of so long a pattern of advancement of leaders from the Economic Department.

This pattern of work with close personal interaction between the staff and senior union officials also points out the force of socialization which draws the organization of the TUC together. Len Murray, his Deputy and Assistant General Secretaries and the Department Secretaries work very well together. There is a high degree of camaraderie and loyalty. All of them have spent years together at the TUC. They do not socialize so much as American colleagues do in their off hours, but there is a special bond of common identification and purpose which serves the organization quite well. The task for creating a coherent trade union government at the centre of so loose a federation would be impossible without such dedication and skill.

4. CONCLUSION

This governing process at the TUC therefore really has two very different faces. One is quite positive and remarkably effective and the other is weak, ineffective and quite sad. The Bill Callaghans, David Leas, Len Murrays, Ken Grahams and Michael Walshes of the TUC staff, to name a few, are top flight administrators. They are certainly every bit as talented as their counterparts in government and private enterprise, and in some ways their deeply-held commitments to trade unionism makes them even more effective. It is their work, to be sure, that causes the Trade Union Congress to function very smoothly and effectively in the administration of its day-to-day responsibilities. This means that the TUC is every bit the central spokesgroup for the trade union movement on an enormously wide range of issues.

Yet it is the other 'face' of the TUC which proves so crucial for its impact on the great issues of the day. One of the major achievements of the TUC staff is that it literally 'wins' the right to administer so effectively on the routine issues which the TUC must face. The General Secretary leads the political bargaining within the General Council which he uses to keep his lead within that body. At the same time, his subordinates are doing just about the same thing in their areas of responsibilities, such as on the individual committees. But their efforts have serious limits. They reach out to control and direct as much as they can. But when issues are more sensitive or stressful, as wage restraint has been, the TUC staff finds it nearly impossible to follow the same leadership pattern. In those cases, union leaders 'take back' the prerogatives which are rightfully theirs and the staff becomes very much their servants about what will be done or not done.

The TUC's organizational structure and decision-making process expresses how the union movement has tried to overcome this problem. Union leaders do participate in an interlocking directorate with the General Secretary and his staff to maximize the chances that they will be able to produce focused and coherent leadership. In many ways, this approach does help the TUC to reach and implement decisions that go beyond the lowest common denominator or are at least at the lowest common denominator when they might not have been achieved at all. But the harsh reality, which has been demonstrated time after time is that the second 'face' tends to dominate in a destructive way. This is a pessimistic commentary which is particularly relevant to any speculation about how the TUC will fare in its efforts to hold the influence and access of trade unionism in a post-collective era.

3 The Politics of Failure: the 'Winter of Discontent', 1978–9

The 'winter of discontent' is a vivid example of the failure of trade union purpose. It would be hard to write a fictional account which better shows the problem of collectivist politics in contemporary Britain. The events of 1979 demonstrated again how negatively powerful the Trades Union Congress can be in paralyzing the policy intentions of incumbent governments, even a Labour government. But it also showed as never before, how much its negative power is the result of its own internal weakness. The impression which the Trades Union Congress had given in earlier years was that its vetoes of public policy were purposeful actions rejecting views that it could not accept. The events of the 'winter of discontent' revealed that its negative power *can be* the result of confusion, weakness and the paralysis of its own internal decision-making process.

This development expresses the context of a new situation in British politics. Union power to disrupt industrial relations remains as potent as ever. But union power and influence on policy decision-making is being sapped by the weakening economic situation and government's abandonment of the economic contract of 1944. No longer do Labour and Conservative governments promise to manage the economy in order to guarantee full employment or a high and constantly rising standard of living. No longer therefore do they need to bid for the same high level of union cooperation.

The 'winter of discontent' in 1979 was played out in this new context. Full employment was gone and replaced by growing unemployment which weakened, confused and clearly frightened the union movement and its spokesgroup, the Trades

59

Union Congress.[1] Keynesianism was dead, but the TUC did not know what to put in its place. Its great leaders of the early and middle seventies were now retired, but their successors were inexperienced, divided and unsure about how to restore a common trade union purpose.

The actual crisis occurred in a series of several episodes lasting from the late spring of 1978 through to the early spring of 1979. Each episode exposed a number of nerve endings which demonstrated how impotent the relationship between the two sides of the labour movement had become. The TUC found itself buffeted from one set of events to another, reacting to the Government on the one hand and to unruly constituent unions on the other. In sum, the profile of its behaviour was one of weakness and a lack of real purpose.

1. THE BEGINNINGS OF CONFLICT

The potential for a serious conflict between the TUC and the Callaghan Government over the issue of wage restraint was glaringly obvious during the spring and into the summer of 1978. However unthinkable to both sides, it seemed that all the lessons of 1969 were being forgotten. Each side seemed stuck with mutually exclusive policy imperatives and appeared determined to hold their positions come what may. No one wanted a fight, just as no one wanted a fight in 1969.[2] Everyone who might make a difference could see the damage that would be an inevitable consequence. But the whole scenario seemed to be on 'automatic pilot', and so it was to be the tragedy that both sides feared.

The benchmark for the argument was the expiration of the last pay restraint agreement between the TUC and the Government on 31 July 1978.[3] It was about whether and perhaps how to extend the wage agreement that both sides argued during the late spring and into the summer.[4] The TUC was angry about the growing number of unemployed. It was also angry about the dislocation that pay restraint had caused over the previous several years. And there was equivalent disquiet about the loss of influence which TUC leaders felt even more keenly than the slippage in the economic circumstances of their members. From any perspective it was impossible, union leaders felt, to find the basis for further agreement. Their members had made it clear repeatedly that they would not tolerate further wage restraint, and from their perspective they could see no advantage in providing more than a superficial gloss of camaraderie while bringing an end to the formal understanding. The problem, however, was that the Government would never quite take 'no' for an answer.

TUC leaders made the most pointed effort to get their message across at a meeting with the Prime Minister and Chancellor on 18 July.[5] They wanted their Labour compatriots to recognize once and for all that there was to be no agreement and to reconcile themselves to go on from that point. But they did not succeed. Each one of the TUC leaders in turn made the same point to Jim Callaghan but he turned them all back with the assertion that he had to have wage restraint by whatever name they wished to call it. He asserted that the gains that the Government had made for them depended on their cooperation and there was no way to wish away that responsibility.

These arguments had all been heard before. They had also worked before in the annual arguments about wage restraint. Each time since 1976 some sort of agreement had been reached, though each was consecutively weaker and more a finesse than an effective understanding. But this time it seemed that a watershed had been reached. There could be no agreement. Ministers genuinely understood this point, but their self-interest could not entertain such an answer. There had to be a way out! The glue of camaraderie had to be made to hold at least long enough to produce a victory in the election which was certain to be held within the next year.

The 18 July meeting deadlocked on this frustrating note. Neither side gave an inch. It was clear that further talks would do no good. Each side would have to go its own way in the hopes that the other would adjust its behaviour enough to inflict as little punishment as possible.[6]

It was equally obvious that the only leverage still available in these circumstances was the common threat of an election which always hung over the incumbency of the minority Government. Whatever their unhappiness, the mere whiff of an election still produced spasms of loyalty by trade unionists which well exceeded the rewards of self-interest which another Labour victory might produce. But given this reaction, it was a 'card' which the Government could manipulate and subsequently did manipulate in the weeks ahead.

2. THE WHITE PAPER OF 21 JULY 1978

The best indication that serious conflict might grow out of the deadlock over pay occurred very soon after the 18 July meeting. The Government decided to take the consequences and issue its planned White Paper stating what the Government wanted wage restraint to be for the following year.[7] This action genuinely surprised the TUC because its leaders had expected that the Government would not want to produce a confrontational situation.[8] That it took such an approach was especially worrisome to them because the now-stated five per cent norm seemed so patently ridiculous. They could reach no other conclusion than that the Government had decided to let the chips fall where they might and therefore to take the consequences for any conflict that might develop.

The only other explanation, or so the thinking went at Congress House, was that the Prime Minister really didn't plan to press this unrealistic policy except to the extent that it fit into an election strategy.[9] Since they believed that the Prime Minister and the Chancellor both were rational, skilful politicians then it must be, they reasoned, that they were preparing for an early election. Then, once they were reconfirmed in office, it must also be that they intended to modify their policy on pay restraint to square with a new policy tolerant of pay rises that could be at the ten per cent level of the present round. Thus, the best approach for the TUC seemed to be to make it clear that they were rejecting the Government's White Paper while offering support and especially encouragement for a fall election.[10]

These musings and the policy conclusions they engendered were encouraged in practical terms by the information which the TUC staff gained from contacts with civil servants and junior ministers. The bulk of these contacts seemed to suggest that an election was indeed in the works.[11] There was a good deal of the usual contradictory chatter about this subject but since it fit the apparently rational explanation for the Government's White Paper, the TUC staff was inclined to accept its validity. After all, the Prime Minister himself would be one of the first to want to avoid a confrontation which he had counseled Wilson and Castle against ten years earlier. In addition, both the Prime Minister and the Chancellor kept repeating in private that they 'understood' the political situation within the union movement and therefore the impossibility of reaching the sorts of agreements that had been concluded two and three years earlier. This 'understanding' when added to the other intelligence suggested to many in the union leadership that the ministers were giving them a knowing wink that everything would be all right.[12]

The General Council, at Len Murray's recommendation, took no chances at any rate. It stated its opposition to the White Paper in strong terms and in public. The stakes were simply too high and the potential for miscalculation too great for them to put all of their influence into private conversations. So they issued a particularly pointed and definitive reply.[13] The statement said that while the TUC shared the Government's 'determination to win the battle against inflation' it 'did not accept the Government's view on how this can be achieved'.[14] In particular, it pointed especially to its conviction, stated clearly to the Government a year earlier, that it was not necessary or wise to set standards for pay settlements. Instead, it argued, it was necessary to set pay through collective bargaining so that the settlements reflected the circumstances in particular companies, industries or services. 'The General Council are disappointed at the Government's lack of confidence in the ability and willingness of trade unionists and employers to deal with these problems in a way which will avoid the emergence of further difficulties, and at the Government's failure to concentrate its effort instead on creating a climate in which responsible bargaining could play a constructive role in further improving economic performance.'[15]

3. THE PHONY ELECTION AND ITS CONSEQUENCES

The Prime Minister's reaction was to play the 'election card'. There has been considerable and unresolved debate about the whole episode of the 'phony' election at the beginning of September 1978. Whatever the reasons why the Prime Minister first encouraged and later backed out of an election, he *did* specifically encourage election fever at the TUC Congress.[16] Whether he cynically planned his strategy that way, the excitement did accomplish the trick of turning the Congress away from its apparent destiny. Instead of spending days criticizing the Government and its five per cent pay norm, the Congress moved away from a mood of anger and conflict toward a celebration of the Government's incumbency and the person of Jim Callaghan.[17] Even the media joined with the delegates in reaching the seemingly certain conclusion that the Prime Minister had come to Congress to start his campaign, and that the start was on a very high note indeed. The *Guardian*, for example, concluded that 'Mr James Callaghan effectively launched his general election campaign yesterday in the euphoric atmosphere of the Trades Union Congress . . .' and that 'Seasoned political hands left the debate on Labour's future convinced that the general election will be announced very soon, possibly after tomorrow's Cabinet meeting. . . .'[18]

This kind of report together with the atmosphere of excitement which was televised nationally from the Congress was a real triumph. For that moment, it washed away the bitterness and rancour and the overriding public impression that the unions and their Government were about to have a falling out. But the glow of that success proved to be short-lived and expensive. Once the Prime Minister, a few days later, told the same journalists that there was *not* to be an election, the backlash against his administration and himself personally by angry trade unionists was much worse than the success he had enjoyed.

Union leaders quite simply felt used by the Prime Minister.[19] Rumours flew thick and fast that he had really made his decision against an election back in mid-August. Whether true or not, the rumours stirred suspicions that were hard for ministers to eradicate. What made the whole matter more painful was that union leaders especially remembered the dinner they had with the Prime Minister at Number 10 on 1 September, just before Congress opened.[20] On that occasion the Prime Minister had all but told them directly that he would be calling an election.[21] He had specifically asked for their 'fraternal' support. Only the most senior TUC leaders had been invited to that dinner: Lord Allen, Moss Evans, Hugh Scanlon, Geoffrey Drain, David Basnett and Len Murray. All had been enormously flattered by the feeling that they were being brought in to hear confidentially of the beginning of the battle. It was hard for them to believe later that the Prime Minister had 'conned' them that evening but he had been so sure, so confident and then had spoken so dramatically to Congress that it was inconceivable to many of them that he could have found good reason to decide against an election only a few days later.[22]

Moreover, they were especially embarrassed by the extent to which they had offered their personal and union support.[23] They felt that they had gone out on a limb and that to a great extent the Prime Minister's later decision was so demoralizing that it amounted to a betrayal of a tacit understanding. It was now clear to them that the resulting backlash would undermine their own leadership and certainly make it more difficult for them to behave in a consensual way with the Government during the coming weeks. They reasoned that as leaders they would need to be less accommodating and more independent. The still unresolved issues that divided the two would thus become more intractable and dangerous.

It was in this poisoned atmosphere that the battle was joined at the Labour Party Conference in early October 1978. Public and private sparring between both sides continued unabated in the days before the Conference opened. Nothing, it seemed, could forestall the large unions and particularly the Transport Workers from exercising their decisive bloc votes. They were determined to have their say and to hit back at the Government. In policy terms, their purpose was not just to condemn wage restraint but to commit the Party to organize a campaign against it.[24] The unions did, in fact, get their way when the votes were counted. Their success was so decisive that even a resolution generally applauding the Government's overall economic policy which, after all, had brought inflation down from 30 to eight per cent was overwhelmingly defeated.

The Conference had no right to dictate to the Government or the Prime Minister but even so the glare of publicity was potentially very damaging. The nation watched on TV as the recently euphoric trade union movement shouted its anger and threats of rebellion.[25]

Once again, the Prime Minister had to decide how to meet his critics. To the TUC's fury at the White Paper, he had offered an election and then suffered its renewed fury when he changed his mind. His decision then was to get the best national press he could at the time of maximum attention, and later to suffer through any consequences. This time he faced just about the same sort of problem and his decision was also the same – which he was to rue in the months ahead.

His speech to the Conference took the delegates by surprise.[26] In advance of it, the media had speculated from whispers in the hotel lobbies that the Prime Minister would stand defiant and picture himself as the leader of all the people with the responsibilities that this position entailed. But instead, he turned conciliatory. He acknowledged the overwhelming opposition to incomes policy, he acknowledged the difficulty this situation posed for his leadership and then invited the TUC to search with him for a compromise. There should be new talks, he insisted, and without saying so explicitly made it seem that the Government would certainly move away from the position which had engendered such strong un-happiness.

The TUC's initial reaction was renewed enthusiasm.[27] Later, it was to feel that the Prime Minister's speech was another chapter in the sort of manipulation they had resented a month earlier. For his speech to the Conference once again raised the hopes of unionists that the Government would back out of their argument over wage restraint. Even Moss Evans was initially sucked into the excitement, enthusing that the Prime Minister had delivered a very good speech which showed that the incomes policy argument had not destroyed Labour's chances for re-election.[28]

Later, Evans was also to regret his words. Close reading of the speech showed that the Prime Minister had not really retreated from his position one bit in making his pitch for renewed talks. Moreover, Evans was to see on the evening news that the Prime Minister with Denis Healey at his side had gone straight from the rostrum to a television interview in which he reaffirmed quite clearly that he and his Government remained committed to the five per cent norm.[29]

The Prime Minister had once again reached out for the best of both worlds. He had thrown the Conference into optimism by his conciliatory tone and then shown himself in interviews to be the tough 'national' leader looking out for the interests of 'all the people'. This is a cynical interpretation to be sure. But it does conform to the pattern which both Callaghan and Healey followed in the previous months. It also says a great deal about the relative loss of union influence and prestige. The truth was that the Prime Minister never forgot their negative power. Talks to try and find a compromise were necessary in order to forestall the long-term problem that their anger would be converted into real trouble at election time the following year. The Prime Minister thus did genuinely want to repair the special relationship. But the reality was also that the TUC had lost a great deal of power since 1975 when the General Council was the main concern of the Wilson Government. The Prime Minister's interest in 1978 was to deflect trouble from his union partners, not to take their advice too seriously.

It must also be noted that the TUC, for its part, showed how negative, passive and unimaginative it can be about its own interests. Its leadership took an almost purely reactive posture to the Prime Minister's manoeuverings. They hit back effectively at a good strategic place, the Labour Party Conference. But they did almost nothing in a positive way to take advantage of the Prime Minister's almost frenzied wish to reach some sort of economic policy peace with them. With some imaginative effort, they might have concocted important trade-offs to help the Prime Minister in a way that he would have appreciated in terms which might have been of tangible benefit to their needs. After all, from union leader perceptions the continued tenure of a Labour government was still more desirable than a Tory government of the kind Mrs Thatcher seemed to be promising.

This more positive approach should also have been easier to construct than it might seem because the TUC staff and most of its senior leadership did hold personal views which were far more in sympathy with government policies than was publicly understood. On the issue of wage restraint, for example, Len Murray and his staff were considerably more in agreement with the Government than they could ever have openly admitted.[30] Their attitudes could not be translated into TUC policies that 'sold out' union interests obviously, but it did give them the possibility for private understandings and behaviour that was more consensual.

4. NEGOTIATIONS BEFORE CONFLICT

Whatever the psychological 'fall out' from the Party Conference, the hard news was that there would be renewed talks. The Prime Minister did successfully remind everyone that they needed to keep on trying whatever their feelings and the extent of impasse. The prospects for success were not very good taking the goal of a solid agreement on wage restraint. The most that might be achieved was a weak, vague agreement to disagree and to carry on together without conflict. Just such an agreement was produced but the big surprise was that even this lowest common denominator understanding would be too much for the General Council to accept.

The talks in late 1978 took on much of the same mood and direction that the 'In Place of Strife' negotiations took in 1969.[31] The TUC wanted the Government to accept the principle of voluntarism. The TUC wanted the Government to stay out of incomes policy and the Government said that this would be a nice idea if the TUC could demonstrate how it could guarantee that wage restraint would be accomplished in some other way, preferably by the TUC itself. But the TUC would have none of it. It was prices, they argued, that fueled wage inflation and it was therefore about prices that government should concern itself.

This argument was an important one in dividing the views of both sides, but it did express an important political situation within the General Council itself. The TUC negotiators were constrained to an unusual extent. It had been the long-standing practice to give the TUC's elders considerable latitude in bargaining with ministers. There had always been a wide understanding about the thrust of TUC strategy but the Council remained open to considerable persuasion. This was not the case in 1978. Feelings about the pay issue ran so high that at the General Council session of October 25 the members gave an explicit warning to the TUC's top team of Murray, Evans, Duffy, Drain, Allen and Basnett that they were not to attempt to 'smuggle in' a new pay deal.[32] Len Murray, in fact, took the unusual step of making a very strong denial of any new pay deal and emphasized to the group that he well remembered the Congress resolution against pay restraint which he somewhat dramatically said was 'written on his heart'.[33] 'The whole thing,' he insisted, 'is about prices and inflation, as distinct from a pay target.'[34]

The course of the talks thus rested on the outcome of the

clash between disagreement over wage policy and the natural and continuing interest both sides felt in preserving their special relationship. Natural camaraderie won out to produce an agreement but it was only symbolic and lacked significance. Neither side budged from their conflicting positions on the pay norm because they felt they simply could not accept the larger political costs. The agreement provided that the TUC send advice on 'responsible' bargaining to negotiators while the Government made new but weak commitments on prices, pay comparability and the low paid workers. *The Times* commented perceptively that the agreement 'consisted of a series of disconnected statements, some by the Government and some by the TUC, which were aimed at concealing the fact that on the fundamental issues of pay policy the two sides disagree fundamentally'.[35]

But the big surprise in the whole scenario was the reaction of the General Council. On a 14–14 vote, taken on 14 November, the Council in an almost unprecedented action turned down the recommendation of both its negotiating team and the Economic Committee which had also endorsed the agreement. The bitter argument within the Council, even over so weak an agreement, was laid bare for all to see. In a highly unusual statement, Tom Jackson, who was then Chairman of the TUC, attacked those who had opposed the agreement.[36] He particularly singled out Alan Fisher, General Secretary of the National Union of Public Employees whom Jackson accused of voting against his own members' interests: 'Mr Fisher voted against one of the best things which could have happened for his members and could have given him the opportunity to do something about the people at the bottom of the heap, who deserve better treatment than what his left is likely to give them'.[37]

Jackson's outburst made public the growing split which was now too obvious to ignore. Half of the Council wanted or felt obliged to press their wage claims come what may. The other half worried about the consequences of unrestrained bargaining. They worried that TUC influence on the Government would be lost if they did not accept this very modest agreement. They worried that Labour would give way to a vindictive Tory government. And just as importantly, a number of them worried that events were pushing the clock back to 1975 with its nightmarish hyperinflation. Jackson, in denouncing the decision, made this view quite succinctly. He pointed out that during the last 'free for all' he had gotten a 33 per cent increase for his men and then watched as it worked its way through an equal price increase and even worse into the loss of about 25,000 postal jobs.[38] He added bitterly, 'I grow tired of the posturing of those who claim to be socialists, those who claim they have some vision of a more equal society, those who at the same time demand the right to get not just their share but as much as is going for their members'.[39]

This sort of public scolding was as unusual as was the vote in the General Council. Jackson had not taken part in the negotiations since he was not a member of the Neddy (NEDC) six. But he was speaking out for that leadership, demonstrating its anger and frustration at the degree to which they had really lost control.

The vote was a watershed in the long history of incomes policies. Until that time, rebellions of this sort had never occurred in a formal way within the General Council. Congress had expressed its displeasure at incomes policies on several occasions during the sixties. The TUC leadership had often recognized this discontent by backing away from agreements with the government or by coming to modified arrangements and once by allowing shop stewards to destroy agreements on the shop floor. This time, in 1978, the TUC leadership had really tried to follow the same tactic. But the difference was that a much larger bloc, now able to affect the decision, was not willing to play the game anymore.

During the earlier periods, Council members in the great majority agreed with TUC leaders that incomes policies were necessary in order to pave the way for a more healthy and growing economy. Their actions were therefore geared to help the senior leadership find some formula which produced a reasonable incomes policy while not stirring up too threatening a reaction from the membership. This time, in contrast, the Council was not nearly so cooperative. Most of those who voted against the agreement genuinely opposed any further debasement of free collective bargaining. Even the word 'advice' was too strong an impediment.

There is also in this episode of deadlock and therefore rejection by the Council some indication of how politics had changed at the TUC. The hostile attitude of so many to anything which smacked of pay restraint was certainly at the heart of what happened. But it is a little surprising that the negotiators and their allies on the Economic Committee and General Council would have put themselves into a position to take so embarrasing a defeat. The fact that this event was so unusual says a great deal about how much it departed from the usual process. It has been almost axiomatic that the leadership never sticks its neck out. Rather, its approach has been to construct laborious compromises which often produce little more than 'lowest common denominator' decisions. When policies have been more aggressive than that, they have been at least rooted in strong support from the largest unions whose powerful influence has forced the acquiescence of the smaller and weaker unions. In this case, there was division within the large union group and no leadership of substantial personal strength to force anything through by harangue. Given the closeness of the vote, it is clear that the General Council seriously missed its two great leaders of the previous decade, Jack Jones and Hugh Scanlon. It was also obvious that the remaining leadership, including Len Murray, did not do its political spadework very well in 'lining up the ducks'. They should have known that they would win the vote or have known that they should not pose the question. Of course, a case can also be made that the defeat was staged in order to fulfill a process of good faith with the Government. The defeat could thereby demonstrate to senior Labour politicians that no matter how weak an agreement they might reach, the state of affairs within the movement had fallen to the point that there was no use discussing wage policy at all. This theory is plausible but Jackson's outburst and the events that followed during the 'winter of discontent' suggest strongly that TUC leaders did not act to stage the outcome but rather were badly defeated by their own colleagues.

5. THE 'WINTER OF DISCONTENT'

Simply put, the Labour Government should have expected nothing less than they endured during the 'winter of discontent'. The White Paper followed by the TUC Congress, the Labour Party Conference and the rejected agreement with the TUC should have been signals enough. But if that was not enough, there were also the other clear indications of trouble coming out of the union conferences throughout the spring and into the summer, and then the difficult union–employer negotiations which were in full swing in a number of areas. The failure at the General Council in mid-November simply sealed the Government's fate once it chose to 'hunker down' and take the heat come what may. Clearly, it could not expect to count on any further help from the TUC. The die was cast.

Waiting in the wings with smug grins and 'I told you so's' in the House of Commons was the happy band of Tories, just itching for a chance to bring down the fragile Government. They could not have asked for a better script. The trade unions demanded free collective bargaining and found themselves as a result more in agreement on that issue with the Tories than with the Labour Cabinet. Mrs Thatcher and her colleagues enjoyed offering up just what the unions wanted, while reminding the Government that it was doing a good job of demonstrating just what they had preached for four years: that incomes policies and collectivist politics simply cannot work.[40]

It is especially useful to examine the 'winter of discontent' of 1978–9 against the comparative example of the Miners crisis of 1973–4.[41] Both produced general elections and each cost the government its power. Both created widespread disruption of industrial production which touched the lives of large groups in the population even though the Heath crisis was certainly the most pervasive. Both occurred in spite of intensive efforts by each government to prevent trouble and to stop it once it had started. Both involved governments in relatively 'hard' arguments with unions over 'maximum' pay increases. And finally, both governments relied on the Trades Union Congress to settle the conflict and reduce damage from the disruptions.

From the opposite perspective, one major difference between the two crises was the difference of party in office. It is interesting in this respect to compare the impact of Jim Callaghan as a Labour Prime Minister, whom trade unionists respected and personally liked, with that of Edward Heath, whom many union leaders regarded as a thoroughly loathsome individual.

A second important difference between the crises was the difference in leadership of the TUC's largest unions and therefore of the TUC itself. Terry Duffy had replaced Hugh Scanlon for the Engineers and Moss Evans had replaced Jack Jones. Duffy represented an important ideological shift to the right. Evans, though ideologically in agreement with Jones, began as a much less experienced and less influential figure in union and national politics. Moreover, Scanlon and Jones had learned to work together within the TUC in a very important way even while continuing their union and personal rivalries. Evans and Duffy not only refused such a working relationship that could have produced similar leadership, they were hardly on speaking terms.[42] This deficiency left a considerable vacuum in the TUC leadership which was painfully obvious throughout the crisis.[43]

The actual crisis developed during December and into January without any very definite starting point. Unofficial action in the road haulage industry which affected important and vital supplies finally gave a sense of reality to the anticipated trouble which newsmen had been predicting for some weeks. But until early January it all had seemed a bit like the 'phony war' of 1940. There had been a bakers' strike during December but that was quite tame in its impact. No one characterized it as a crisis or as a forerunner to a crisis. There were news reports of difficult and unsuccessful negotiations and continued grumblings about the failure of the TUC to come to agreement with the Government but no one took their attention from the holiday season to look carefully at what was happening. Had the general public been more attentive, they would have seen the signs of trouble everywhere.

There was, however, very serious concern at Congress House, especially by TUC civil servants.[44] The Government and the unions concerned with public services, rail, road haulage and water supply were on a collision course. Negotiations were going nowhere and the clamour to take industrial action was much stronger than they believed the Government really understood. What was so frustrating to them, however, was how helpless they felt in the face of the gathering trouble.

They felt that the failure of the General Council to approve the agreement had just about destroyed the influence they had with Whitehall – and it had done so just when they needed as much influence as possible.[45] At the same time, the rancour produced by that decision had exposed the serious inability of the General Council to deal with real trouble. Clearly the vote had expressed the anger of the membership below and it was equally obvious that if widespread industrial disruptions occurred the union movement was very badly placed at the moment to take action on its own and respond to government pressure. They were convinced that the two sides, Government and TUC, would recognize their common interests in peace. Even the rejected agreement had proved this point. But the TUC civil service couldn't find much hope that the two sides would be able to reconcile their fundamental disagreement on pay or that the TUC would be any more able than before to reach an effective agreement.

They were, in fact, even more pessimistic than they had been because they saw an unusual amount of bitterness developing. Both sides seemed to feel a degree of contempt for the other.[46] The long sessions during the fall which produced so little and then the utter debacle of the General Council's veto had produced a cynicism which could be seen in brief flashes of anger. This had been especially noticeable in the meeting between the Economic Committee and the Chancellor on 19 December.[47] There had been brave words about working together on common objectives but little effort to hide the mutual scepticism that most participants seemed to feel.

There is no doubt that these feelings inhibited and delayed communications and action in January as the crisis developed. Widespread disruptions of supplies and effective secondary picketing brought back memories of 1973–4 shortly after the beginning of the new year. It was not until the Prime Minister had returned from a summit meeting in Guadeloupe on the 10th of January that both sides began to come to grips with the exploding situation.

Even then, it is interesting that the impetus to take action came principally from the Government's reaction to the media and opposition. A reading of the newspapers during the first half of January gives the impression of Britain at disaster's door and a sense that the only cries for rational change and the taming of the union monster were coming from the leader of the opposition, Mrs Thatcher. The Government was pictured as either doing nothing or in paralysis. What is so striking about all this is that the Government itself moved to deal with the situation from this point of reference, acting very much as Mr Heath had by responding to the clamour of media criticism and opposition charges. This tended to supercharge the atmosphere.

Mr Callaghan thus began to lead his Government's responses on his return from Guadeloupe as nearly a prisoner of contextual pressure. And in a style typical of this sort of situation in the postwar collectivist period, he attempted to patch things up as best he could. Patching up in union–labour relations means getting the obvious disruptions ended as fast as possible while trying to construct some form of understanding with the TUC that would not only shore up their willingness and ability to see that it didn't happen again very soon, but also that somehow the special relationship between the two sides was still intact. In this latter way, the Labour Government was obviously different from the Conservatives who had no hope of creating a special relationship and among Mrs Thatcher and her colleagues, little interest in such collectivist deals.

The Government's opening gambit in its effort to patch things up did not go very well in substantive terms, but did create communication channels and sensitivities that were to be useful in later days. On the day after he arrived home from Guadeloupe, the Prime Minister met with both Moss Evans and Len Murray.[48] The subject was the lorry drivers strike and, in particular, the problems of disruptions and what the Transport Workers' attitude was toward the still unofficial action. Later that day, the Chancellor met with the TUC Economic Committee on the same subject.[49] That discussion went much further, however, covering the whole range of current industrial relations. The Government's strategy in both meetings was the same: it wanted Evans to withhold union sanctions for the strike and to promise to get control over unruly secondary picketing. At the same time, it wanted to convince the TUC to take responsibility for applying similar pressure on Evans and to direct efforts at avoiding disruptive problems in the other disputes which were coming to a boil.

The Prime Minister was completely unsuccessful in dealing with Evans. The Transport Workers boss quite pointedly rejected the Prime Minister's views, responding that the pay claim for the lorry drivers was eminently justified.[50] He also insisted that although secondary pickets had been over-zealous, the best way to get control over them was by making the strike official and giving his union the chance to use their influence.[51]

The Chancellor fared no better with the Economic

Committee later in the day. TUC leaders were in 'no mood to be blamed for what they' viewed 'as a crisis brought about by the strict imposition of the Government's' ridiculous '5 per cent pay policy'.[52] Neither warnings of a tough spring budget nor veiled threats of possible legislation against secondary picketing budged union leaders toward cooperation. Instead, the meeting became ugly in personal terms. Finally, Harry Urwin of the Transport Workers, himself in charge of coordinating the drivers strike, bitterly warned the Chancellor that the Government's attitude – especially in thinking about legislation – would provoke just the sort of row that Mr Heath and before him Mr Wilson had experienced.[53]

Both meetings were grim indeed, especially compared to the close union–government relations since Labour returned to office in 1974. Each side was angry at the stubbornness of the other. The long months of negotiations had come to nothing and now they found themselves just where they had vowed ten years earlier never to be again: in serious confrontation and faced with a likely Tory victory in the next election. Yet, the meetings did have an important positive influence because they tended once again to rekindle the familial relationship that operates toward common survival. No one left either meeting feeling very good about the prospects for 'getting out of the situation' without much damage. But those who were there report that there remained that familiar determination to find some way out.[54]

It must have been difficult indeed for any of the participants to concentrate with too much detachment during the following days. The period from 11 to 17 January proved to be the highest point of many high points in the barrage of criticism that the press and the opposition levelled on the Government and the unions. Months later the TUC produced a pamphlet. 'A Cause for Concern', which specifically complained about what the unions believed was totally unfair treatment.[55] Looking at the headlines at that moment and comparing them with those of the Heath period, it seems that in both instances the press spared little imagination in concocting the most dramatic headlines. Of course, British readers have long known that they must discount the headlines they see in their evening newspapers. But by any measurement, the TUC's complaints about this period are certainly justified. The impression that was conveyed was that Britain was on the brink of ruin and that millions would be on the dole in a matter of days. Generally, the tactic of the media was to present projections of possible events and statistics rather than a description of what really was happening. Headlines like 'Shops will soon run out', 'Food stocks will run out – Grocers may close' and '2 million face lay off and soon' were quite common.[56]

At the same time, the Tories quite understandably grabbed this golden opportunity. Mrs Thatcher was quite skilful during this period.[57] She had a number of interviews in the press and on television in which she as well as her colleagues emphasized that these sordid events only confirmed her long-standing criticism that power in industrial relations was sorely out of balance. Mrs Thatcher used several media occasions to offer her specific proposals which, among other things, suggested that the Government provide free postal election and strike ballots, withdraw social security payments for unionists who strike without ballot, and end the right to strike in public utilities. Of course Mrs Thatcher never failed to point out that all of these events demonstrated that Labour governments do not hold the mystical powers to ensure cooperation and peace with the union movement which they smugly advertise.

This Tory approach was quite skilful and set the stage for the pattern of its relationship with the unions once Mrs Thatcher's Government was elected in May 1979. Edward Heath ten years earlier had played on many of the same arguments which Mrs Thatcher used. The difference was that his proposals matched the force of his criticism and his voice was really the only voice speaking for the Tory position. It was therefore much easier for him to make his case against the unions directly, but it was also much easier for the unions to make Heath a direct target. The difference during this latter period was that Mrs Thatcher's words were much harsher than the proposals she made. She had the advantage of hindsight which Heath could not have enjoyed and therefore she could appear firm but reasonable to the electorate and to a number of unionists who were not sympathetic to the events which were unfolding.

She also had the help of a skilful colleague, which Mr Heath never really permitted. James Prior was the Conservative spokesman on employment. He carefully trod the role of moderate pro-unionist with the explicit task of mollifying union concern. He did his job so well at the time that to at least a few trade unionists he seemed almost preferable to their brethren on the political side of the labour movement.[58]

It is always a subjective judgment as to what effect all of this publicity had on the events that occurred but it seems fair to say that they had a very great impact. A kind of restrained panic gripped Congress House as well as Whitehall. Whatever the more dispassionate public remarks that brave ministers made in an effort to tone down the situation, the meetings of the Cabinet during this period clearly revealed the extent of their real concern and fear about the impact of the strikes on the electorate. Everyone was agreed that the press and the opposition were blowing the whole situation out of proportion. But nonetheless, they were also aware that the publicity was having its effect. Had they any doubt, they only had to remember, after all, that they had used very similar circumstances in 1974 against the Heath Government. Their victory in the February 1974 election – though on a minority decision – still demonstrated the powerful effect that public relations could have. Therefore, their reaction in 1979 was to treat the situation with as much panic as the media and the opposition portrayed even while complaining that the publicity was overblown and unfair. The result was to produce hyperactivity, with the Government wanting to be seen in command, accomplishing dramatic progress toward a temporary and then permanent solution not just of the current disruptions, but of the 'union problem'. Once in full swing, particularly from mid-January to mid-February, the feeling of activity even became a tonic unto itself. There developed a school of thought which suggested that all of these troubles would prove to be the great leverage leading to victory at the polls.

The beginning of hyperactivity can clearly be marked as the debate in the House of Commons on 16 January on a Tory motion for adjournment which had been downgraded at the last moment from a full-scale debate on a motion of no confidence in the Government's handling of the crisis. The Tories were still confident that they held the edge in the argument but they decided that it would be strategically wiser to stage their attack from the tamer confines of an adjournment motion. The votes were just not there to embarass the Government and certainly not to defeat it at the moment.

Mrs Thatcher's attack followed fairly much the same line that she had taken for the previous three weeks.[59] She was indignant about the disruptions caused by unruly pickets and sharply critical of what she described as government inaction. She insisted that the Government should move quickly and firmly to adopt policies which would deal with the abuses of the closed shop, impose a picketing law and provide for secret ballots. If Mr Callaghan would promise all these things, she could promise that her colleagues would support his Government wholeheartedly.

In reply, Mr Callaghan was not much interested in Mrs Thatcher's support.[60] His speech concentrated instead on blending a criticism of picketing practices with reassurances that the situation was nowhere as bad as the opposition leader would want people to believe. However, he said that there was a balance in society between the undeniable right of people to withdraw their labour and the rights of the community against all sectional interests. This meant that in the road haulage dispute the drivers needed to measure their grievances against the effect industrial action was having on the whole of society. But the bottom line in taking action still rested with the drivers and their unions because the Prime Minister believed that voluntary compliance out of a sense of decent conduct was far better than any laws which would be only of secondary value. The Government, he said, did intend to draw up a code of conduct although he was reluctant to see it legally imposed.

The Prime Minister then turned to the overriding issue of his Government's pay policy. He repeated his well known position that the Government would not retreat in order to allow a return to the high inflation of three years earlier. However, he did announce a new flexibility which he obviously hoped would have a salutary impact on the crisis, particularly on the growing threat of a public service workers walkout. He announced that the Government would allow lower paid workers, who would be defined as those making less than £60 per week (up from the old figure of £44.50), to be paid an increase of at least £3.50 per week even though this would violate the five per cent norm.[61] In addition, the Government would be agreeable to the principle of comparability in public sector pay with that of the private sector. He promised that the Government would move to establish the necessary mechanism to provide for such a review and that the results would be implemented in stages. Finally, he added that the Government planned to introduce a bill that would allow the Price Commission to restrict price increases. The Commission previously had been prohibited from vetoing price rises based exclusively on increased costs.

Throughout his presentation the Prime Minister was a studied contrast to Mrs Thatcher. He was avuncular where she had been sharp and biting. His delivery was slow and careful while hers had been at machine-gun speed. One could almost imagine that they were talking about a completely different state of affairs, one serious and out of control, the other significant but well within the grasp of the solution. Each obviously was filling a purposeful role. But even the Prime Minister at certain moments showed the strain of the situation. He was clearly speaking well beyond his audience, not so much to the electorate, which was obviously in his mind, but to the TUC.

The Prime Minister was sending a variety of messages. The most important message was that he wanted to go all-out to deal with the crisis. He wanted the TUC to take up the challenge to press the Transport Workers and he wanted Moss Evans to get control of his union. Both messages had been conveyed before but without impression. He wanted both to know that the pressure for declaring a State of Emergency could not be resisted forever nor did he believe that he should resist for long. He wanted to tell his union colleagues that he was willing to support collective bargaining and that he knew a price had to be paid, but that *they* had to pay a price too. He wanted them to know that the five per cent norm could be breached on the edges but not in its substance, at least to the extent that agreements not sabotage the economic programme upon which he felt the future viability of his Government depended. And finally, he wanted to signal that these matters needed to be sorted out in real terms and a start made to reach agreement that would head off both a public service workers debacle and continued long-term strife. There, for all to see, was a carrot and a stick for the unions. The Prime Minister offered collaboration and attention to union concerns, but he wanted to cut the losses immediately and to shore up the alliance for the future.

Confirmation that these were his purposes came very quickly, as did confirmation of its effect. Callaghan showed he still held considerably more influence than Wilson had in a comparable crisis. While newspaper articles about 'disaster gripping the country' reached a crescendo during the following two days, the Prime Minister held additional meetings and telephone calls with Moss Evans and other TUC leaders. The TUC also geared up its own internal consultation process. His message was quite simply that the strikes, particularly the lorry drivers' strike, was literally killing the Government and playing into the hands of the Tories. And the additional message was that unless they could act more vigorously to control secondary picketing the Government would have no recourse but to declare the State of Emergency that they had so far held off. If he were to take such an action, he warned, he would need to bring in troops to deal with the situation. His pressure was intense and the reaction received included both resentment and considerable worry. Evans, who was the object of the meetings and telephone calls, came to resent bitterly the pressure which he felt was totally unreasonable.[62] His TUC colleagues generally did not like the pressure either but they were considerably more in favour of some sort of cooperation.[63] Thus, after Callaghan talked with Evans and Murray on 17 January at Number 10, the TUC's most senior members met as the Finance and General Purposes Committee to discuss the strike.

This session on 18 January was particularly stormy.[64] Evans took the brunt of a good deal of tough talk about the ability of his unions to control secondary pickets. Len Murray had already signalled his own concern about this matter on the previous day at the meeting with the Prime Minister and to the press. His main purpose was to keep control of the situation within the union movement on a voluntary basis as opposed to any sort of government intervention.[65] He had spent a great number of hours during the previous week trying to hold the bridge against a growing sentiment within the Cabinet for the declaration of a State of Emergency. Thus, at the meeting of the General Purposes Committee, Murray and the others were anxious to thrash out an understanding with Evans about shoring up efforts to get the situation under control.

The problem for the participants was the fear of a watershed breach in the principle of voluntarism. After all, governments over the last ten years had made several serious attempts ('In Place of Strife' and the Industrial Relations Act to name the most significant) to legislate control over industrial relations. The argument from governments to both parties had been that whatever the value of voluntarism, its credibility as an effective principle was very little in the face of widespread industrial disruption. Now, with a Labour government in trouble, and headed by a Prime Minister who had supported voluntarism so vigorously, it was crucial to TUC leaders that they be seen as able to demonstrate their authority. To do otherwise was to invite legislation now and much worse legislation when the apparently inevitable Tory victory occurred.

Evans was angry at being tagged with the 'bad guy' image but he could not ignore the pressure.[66] It was not so much the argument about saving the Labour Government as the complaints that the strike was harming so many hundreds of thousands of other unionists who were not involved.[67] That latter point really touched his sensitivities. Thus, in response, he proceeded to issue revised guidelines on picketing. Although he carefully described them as 'recommendations', they firmly instructed his membership that TGWU officials would decide where pickets would be stationed. Also he made it clear that the number of pickets would be limited exclusively to those who were members of the union and clearly identified as such.

A day later, the Government quickly expressed 'satisfaction' with the new 'recommendations' sent out by the TGWU.[68] The Prime Minister told the Commons that 'at the moment' he was willing to give the code a chance to work since it would be far better it if was maintained by the TGWU. In the days that followed, the press kept a careful scorecard on the success of the TGWU effort. Although there were still many stories about disruptions, the code did have a favourable impact.

More importantly though, Evans also succeeded in encouraging more fruitful and intense negotiations. Gradually, the strike began to wind down as individual settlements were reached. It is interesting to note that the terms of those settlements provided for pay rises of about 15 per cent, or about three times above the government norm. But by this time the attention of the participants, the public and even ministers tended to stray away from the terms of the agreement in favour of an overwhelming desire that order and business return to normal. No one said it publicly, but the clear sentiments by those concerned directly and the public at large was that the terms could be whatever it took – a not too unfamiliar attitude to those who remembered the course of the Miners' Strike in 1974. The Prime Minister thus made his influence felt but at a price he had steadfastly refused to pay. The Labour Government had once again shown the power of familial relations but to what good effect?

6. THE 'WINTER OF DISCONTENT' UNRESOLVED

The winding down of the lorry drivers' strike did not by any means spell the beginning of peace on the industrial relations front. If anything, it proved to be the first and easiest chapter in a longer drama that was to play out throughout the rest of the winter leading to the Government's defeat in the House of Commons on 28 March. The dispute over pay for public service workers, which had been festering for some time, heated up immediately and was even more difficult because it involved the Government directly. The TUC had indeed promised and delivered its support against the picketing chaos in the lorry drivers' strike. But the argument over the pay norm was a much tougher issue and the lorry drivers' pay settlement certainly provided no help to the Government at all.

The difference by this point in late January was that the TUC and the Government were now willing to join in serious negotiations about the crisis. This had certainly not been the case when the Prime Minister returned from Guadeloupe only 12 days earlier. At that time, the sessions with the Chancellor or Prime Minister were still mainly ugly exchanges about who was to blame for the trouble. Now, the situation had changed. On the union side, the important difference was the threat of widespread and serious industrial disruption affecting a large number of workers not involved in the disputes.[69] The political threat to the Labour Government was also a compelling argument for cooperation, but probably not much more than it had been at the time that the General Council deadlocked during the fall. It was thus the industrial threat now which propelled even the leaders of Britain's largest unions to want the TUC to take the lead in negotiating both some sort of peace for the chaotic industrial situation as well as a more permanent arrangement to forestall such problems in the future.

This situation was a classic prescription for imporant change in TUC governance. It has historically been only at moments of the gravest crisis and threat that constituent unions have been willing even to consider ceding portions of their authority to a central directing force. Len Murray has long recognized this point and in the winter of 1979 he attempted to seize on the opportunity to make important gains. The ultimate defeat of the Labour Government at the hands of the House of Commons in March aborted much of the change but the accomplishments during late January and early February in negotiations for a new agreement with the Government were important milestones. The media tended to miss the significance of these changes as it focused instead on the negotiations as little more than a superficial rescue attempt for the Government – which it was in part.

One of the key indications that Murray was trying to seize the initiative was that he personally became more involved in individual disputes than he had at any time during his tenure as General Secretary. His efforts went beyond the two major public service and lorry drivers' disputes to the less threatening but still serious problems with the trainmen and workers in the water supply industry. He proved to be quite skilful and won a great deal of personal praise for his work. He was not completely successful in each case, but he was generally able to keep matters from getting out of control. In the rail dispute, for example, he succeeded in defusing a serious disagreement between two unions who were about to go to 'war' with each other. But even more importantly, he was able to convince individual union leaders that the situation was so fraught with danger that they should even risk running afoul of their membership in seeking rapid and peaceful settlements.

Murray's major effort, however, was to get the TUC into renewed negotiations with the Government and then to guide them to a wide-ranging agreement which would provide new powers to forestall this sort of crisis in the future. David Basnett and Lord Allen were key figures who helped Murray in this work. Basnett especially believed that the alliance with Labour was indispensible to union interests and he made a special effort to ignite a new round of talks.[70] The table below documents the number and frequency of the meetings between both sides:

Formal TUC–Government contacts from 23 January to 9 February 1979

23 January	Liaison Committee meets at Congress House.
26 January	TUC Economic Committee meets with Chancellor and other Economic Ministers.
29 January	TUC General Council meets with Prime Minister. TUC Employment and Policy Committee meets

	with Employment Secretary and other ministers.
31 January	TUC Economic Committee meets with Chancellor and other Economic Ministers.
1 February	TUC Employment and Policy Committee meets with Employment Secretary and other ministers.
5, 7, 9, 14 February	Joint meetings, including TUC Economic Committee and Employment and Policy Committees meeting with Prime Minister and other ministers.

The negotiations operated on several levels, revealing a great deal about the distribution of power within the TUC. At the top of the pyramid, senior TUC leaders and especially Len Murray freely consulted with and even bargained with government ministers including the Prime Minister himself. These contacts have been part of every negotiation between the government and the TUC over the years. The difference in this case was that they were more frequent and more personal.[71] Murray clearly took the lead. He tried to guide the pattern of behaviour within TUC institutions in order to construct a coherent and viable policy that would not suffer another intra-TUC defeat. At the same time, he tried to educate ministers about the limits of TUC compromise and to otherwise put them in a mood to soften their obvious impatience and frequent disdain. In sum, Murray and to some extent Allen and Basnett became the key arbitrators in the scenario.

At the next level, General Council members were kept actively informed and care was taken to consult with them about the state of negotiations. Murray had several of his most trusted deputies take on this responsibility. Part of this task was intertwined with the responsibility that the Economic Committee and Employment Policy and Organization Committee held in the talks. The chairman and members of these committees were, of course, also members of the General Council and their participation was vital to what happened.

The November débâcle was a compelling lesson which hung over the course of the January/February bargaining.[72] Negotiators were careful to avoid any hint of an incomes policy. The goal from the beginning was to do their job well enough so that the General Council would acquiesce in the agreement without a formal vote. That had also been the strategy in November but the negotiations engendered so much publicity about the pay norm that many union leaders began to feel they had to go on record in opposition. The potential for another row was certainly present, though there seemed broad agreement that everything should be done to avoid another public embarrassment.

It needs to be added, however, that for a fleeting moment in late January it looked as if this strategy would come unraveled. Twelve moderate and right-wing members of the General Council decided to go ahead and issue recommendations they had been working on for some months to deal with the overall problem of wage restraint, as a solution to the deadlock that had festered for so long.

The group included some of the TUC's most powerful leaders who were otherwise engaged in the negotiations with the government. Lord Allen, Frank Chapple, Terry Duffy and Tom Jackson were among the most prominent. Their statement, *The Better Way,* proposed a full blown, formal and permanent incomes policy.[73]

The proposal consisted of six recommendations. The most important was the proposal for an annual economic discussion between government, business and unions each year at which an 'indicative norm' would be agreed for pay rises.[74] In addition, they proposed that the TUC be able to give advice in individual cases where pay settlements are in dispute; that something like the old Prices and Incomes Board be recreated to advise firms on the effect that pay agreements would have on the overall prices and dividends picture; that government take tough action to freeze or cut prices; and finally that there be an investigation of the role of profits with an eye to worker profit sharing. This approach, they felt, would defuse the resentment created after pay settlements which subsequently allowed the business involved to make huge profits.

The proposals were not startling nor revolutionary but they did raise initial fears that there would be a new wave of intra-union dissension. This potential seemed real because they were issued on the very day that the General Council met with the Prime Minister. But the effect proved to be the opposite. There certainly was some resentment by more militant Council members who seemed especially irked that the group of twelve took the bold step of publicly airing so important a split in their ranks.[75] But the general reaction was very mild tending toward a positive feeling that the proposals contained elements about which both sides might be able to agree without even touching the worst problem of the five per cent norm.[76] After all, it was the norm that caused most of the problem. Discussions about the wage issue that were off-limits until now could be resumed if they were deflected onto other aspects of the question. As it turned out then, the recommendations by the right–moderate group did help the negotiations, especially as the mild reaction of all concerned seemed to indicate how anxious even the most militant leaders were to reach some sort of agreement.

The actual work toward an agreement was done by the two committees that operated at the bottom of the policy-making pyramid: the Economic Committee and the Employment and Organization Committee. The Economic Committee certainly holds the greater prestige and influence. Economic policy is always a key element in the TUC's work, and the Committee's importance is matched by the importance of the leaders who are its members. The Employment and Organization Committee, by comparison, deals more with industrial relations and intra-union affairs. These are certainly vital matters but its membership had traditionally been composed of leaders of smaller unions as well as deputy leaders of the larger unions. At this time, Lord Allen was chairman of the Economic Committee and Harry Urwin, the deputy at the Transport Workers, headed Employment and Organization

For the first half of the talks the two committees met separately with Ministers. The Economic Committee met with the Chancellor and other economic ministers while Employment and Organization met with the Employment Secretary and other related ministers. Toward the conclusion of the discussions, from 7 February onward, the two committees met jointly with the Government. By and large, the Economic Committee talked and negotiated about the general outlines of the relationship, particularly concerning inflation, general economic policy and the role of pay.[77] The other committee dealt entirely with the conduct of industrial relations and most particularly with the suggested code of practice which the Employment Minister proposed. Once joint sessions were established, the two areas were merged so that the final agreement concerned the full range of issues between both sides.

Things went smoothly once it was well accepted by both sides that there could be no talk of a prescribed incomes policy and especially the five per cent norm. There certainly was a good deal of haggling about philosophy and detail. The major job was to find a way to state irreconcilable differences in a consensual manner while also posing the trade-offs each side would receive for its agreement.[78]

The Government wanted the TUC's commitment for a code of industrial practice more than it wanted any other concession.[79] It would have liked something on economic policy and pay but that issue was already hopeless. The TUC especially wanted something on prices, which it could point to as providing solid evidence that the Government had union interests at heart.[80] The Economic Committee had held throughout that the only real way to get the restraint of wages which the Government wanted so fervently was by the restraint of prices and therefore the lowering of rates of inflation. The final statement of agreement, which was approved or more accurately 'acquiesced in' on 14 February by the General Council patched all of these things together.[81]

The agreement was more important than its critics allowed but it was as sad a commentary on the state of collectivist politics and the weakness and confusion of the TUC as they complained. It is all a matter of perspective, particularly the perspective of short versus long-term development.

The short-term perspective on the agreement is much more positive than the media and opposition admitted. With crisis at hand, both sides did recognize their need to 'hang together rather than hang separately'. This principle was quite sensible in this context. The Government and unions, after all, did have a real stake in Labour's re-election. Their conflict did produce destructive effects even on the memberships of unions which were not involved. The five per cent norm was unrealistic whatever the Government's political imperatives and a way therefore had to be found to finesse the problem. And finally, they were quite right in addressing the TUC's serious and defective inability to control the sort of industrial chaos which occurred during the 'winter of discontent'. The instructions which the General Council voted to send to its member unions were a gain for TUC authority and may be useful to a future Labour government in perhaps forestalling some of the worst problems of 1979.

All of these things were real gains that together made the agreement more significant than it seemed. The crisis was resolved with help from the TUC. And yet, from a longer term and larger perspective, the crisis and subsequent agreement did little to resolve the problem of collectivist politics in Britain.

First, the TUC showed again that as a powerful producing group it can decide to frustrate, paralyze and even veto official government policy. Second, this episode especially demonstrated that the inherent weakness of the TUC *can cause it to lose the power to decide anything.* In this case, the union movement delivered its powerful influence in the form of a 'winter of discontent' in spite of the objections of a great many individual union leaders and the collective disapproval of the TUC itself. Third and finally, the TUC in these negotiations demonstrated that it could not decide what it really wanted to gain. Faced with dissension in its own ranks and the threat and later actual rebellion of its membership, the TUC lost its policy perspective which became at times no more than a desperate wish to restore peace and thereby its authority. The influence it finally wielded in settling the dispute came at the most extreme moment when panicked union leaders agreed to contribute some of their authority in a desperate attempt to stop the chaos which was directly harming their own members. While the TUC did gain by its new writ of authority, the manner and circumstances of that gain show how unwilling its constituent unions are to fundamentally rebalance the situation. This is a pessimistic commentary on the TUC's future prospects.

7. SNATCHING DEFEAT FROM THE JAWS OF VICTORY

None of these pessimistic assessments was allowed to creep into the official reaction of either side to the agreement. There was genuine pleasure and especially relief that they had wiped away the blot of the November débâcle. There was also, though, awareness that this gain needed to be used as momentum and argument to settle the remaining industrial disputes which could explode to wreck the situation once again.

The local authority workers in the public sector posed the most serious problem. Len Murray as well as the Prime Minister devoted nearly all of their time in the following days to an effort to solve the dispute. It was a frustrating and disappointing struggle, which ultimately showed how vulnerable both were to the weakness of the trade union movement as a collectivity.

The Prime Minister hoped he could score a breakthrough by compromising his pay policy. His 'sweetener' was to add to the basic pay offer a promise of establishing an Independent Standing Commission to study comparative pay between the public sector and the private sector.[82] Depending on the findings of that commission, the pay of public workers could increase in two instalments, one in August 1979 and the other in April 1980. The increments that might be gained at that time could be considered as outside the government's policy and thus not limited as to amount.

This seemed at Congress House to be a significant improvement which should at least have been the basis for a settlement. But such was not to be the case. While the top leadership of the four unions involved were generally favourable to the proposal, dissension within the executive committee of the largest, the National Union of Public Employees (NUPE), proved to be devastating.

At the beginning of March, the TUC and the Government watched in despair as the NUPE membership formally voted to take the advice of their executive and continue the strike.[83] In doing so, they rebuffed their own General Secretary, Alan Fisher, the TUC General Secretary, the leaders of every major trade union and the Prime Minister. To the public at large the Government still seemed unable to get matters under control – right up until the day it lost the vote of censure in the House of Commons. The public service dispute continued to fester throughout the election campaign and died out only when it no longer mattered to the defeated Government.

8. CONCLUSION

The final years of the Labour Government thus proved to be a first and distressing test of TUC behaviour in the new era of post Keynesian economic management. The ineffectiveness of the TUC leadership as the central union spokesgroup had contributed importantly to the failure of collectivist politics,

Britain's continuing economic difficulties and the attack on union power which it now suffered. The prospects that it could rally to fend off its loss of influence and its members' loss of their jobs was always doubtful. The course of the events leading up to and including the 'winter of discontent' showed this pessimism to be well founded. Not only was the TUC inherently unequal to the task for the same reasons that it experienced in the crisis, but the stresses of those events 'cracked' even the limited effectiveness which TUC leaders had carefully drafted into their decision-making process.

The dilemma posed by the 'winter of discontent' was the same as the dilemma faced by union leaders for many years, except that it was more stressful in the post-Keynesian context. The Labour Government, on the one hand, insisted that the TUC deliver effective, fraternal cooperation on issues which naturally exacerbate fissures within the trade union movement. But it made its demands without arming the TUC with countervailing gains which it could use as evidence to its membership that new sacrifices for this Government would be rewarding. At the same time, the TUC's constituent unions were encouraging the trade union centre to resist with great strength government's demands which they felt were unreasonable and undermined their own internal political positions. Yet, as usual, these constituent unions were not willing to contribute their authority to enhance the TUC's ability to deliver on their demands. Quite to the contrary, individual unions at this time made their demands for TUC strength while they more vigorously protected their individual interests from the intrusion of unfavourable economic circumstances.

The TUC was clearly caught in the middle of this pull and tug. Post-Keynesian politics was demanding that it be more powerful in all directions, but the reality was that it had never been powerful or purposeful enough and the prospects were that it would be even less equal to the challenge in the future.

4 The Politics of Continuing Failure: the Beginning of the Thatcher Government, 1979–80

Despair is the emotion which Mrs Thatcher's election as Prime Minister evoked at the Trades Union Congress.[1] This was no ordinary change of government. Its leaders knew that Mrs Thatcher came to office with an avowed anti-collectivist purpose of ending trade union participation in national policy-making. They despaired for their 'contributions' to the Conservative victory, and for their fear that Mrs Thatcher would succeed in her anti-collectivist purpose.

It was hard for union leaders to accept this situation for what it was. Barely more than five years before they had euphorically celebrated the defeat of Mr Heath. Coming after their earlier victory over Harold Wilson and then against the Industrial Relations Act, it had seemed to TUC leaders that the 1974 struggle would likely be the last for a long time to come. No politician in his right mind, they reasoned, would soon risk another assault on the 'right' of trade unionism to influence the course of public policy, and especially economic and industrial policy.[2]

Looking back from mid-1979, it therefore seemed that everything imaginable had gone wrong during the intervening years to contribute to Mrs Thatcher's new and much more dangerous challenge. Intense economic crisis and particularly hyperinflation had provoked the predecessor Labour Government to change the terms of economic management in a way which directly undermined union power. Gradually the TUC had lost important influence. Resulting dissension along with the retirement of key union leaders had added impetus to the decline. And the 'winter of discontent' had exposed the weakness and confusion of the union movement and particularly its spokesgroup, the Trades Union Congress.

Mrs Thatcher started with these undeniable advantages. She also began with a personal and political determination to succeed where Mr Heath had failed. The key questions therefore focused on whether the union movement could rally to meet her inevitable challenge. Could the Trades Union Congress marshall the ideas, the leadership and the organizational strength to turn back her 'attack'?

The course of the interaction between the TUC and the new Thatcher Government during its early months in office did much to answer these questions. And most of the answers were in the negative. It gradually became obvious that the fate of this Conservative Government would depend far more on the success or failure of its policies than any influence which the trade union movement might exert.

1. CONSERVATIVE GOVERNMENT AND THE UNIONS

The Trades Union Congress historically has been of two minds about the election of a Conservative government. On the one hand, the TUC has feared the arrival in office of what their leadership regards as class enemies. Conservative ministers to them are almost invariably distant, aloof and hostile and often dedicated to damaging the interests of trade unionism. They also bemoan their loss of positive influence on the development of public policy, while worrying that Conservative government will busy itself with punitive legislation.

On the other hand, the Trades Union Congress has often secretly welcomed the return of the Tories to office.[3] There is first of all their relief at being rid of a Labour government. Labour governments always seem to demand and expect cooperation from their allies in the labour movement. They may not enjoy similar good fellowship or an identity of policy views with Conservative governments but at least they 'enjoy' the absence of familial relations. Their fundamental incompatibility with Tories has allowed them historically to refuse collaboration and thus to be negatively influential in a way that they could not be with

Labour.[4] Stalemate, policy paralysis and policy veto are all much more available to them in this context than with Labour in office. They have been able to refuse cooperation and even gain political advantage by their negative behaviour because they could at least always count on the support of their own membership. Tory bashing, in fact, has been good medicine for any union leader who found his credibility slipping.[5]

The Tories' view of trade unionism, by comparison, obviously has been quite different. They have also feared the relationship but gained no countervailing advantage from it.

The origins of the Tory view are to be found in the General Strike of 1926. It had been 'their' Government that had defeated the Trades Union Congress and the Miners but the legacy of that experience had proved almost entirely negative for them. The problem was that a whole generation of Tory politicians became impressed with the enormous disruptive power of the trade union movement.[6] This impression was not so relevant to their behaviour during the balance of the interwar years when deprivation had the upper hand, but it became very relevant in the postwar collectivist period.

Winston Churchill was the key figure in molding Conservative postwar relations with the unions. He had been one of those most worried by the events of 1926. Later, as wartime Prime Minister he was careful to develop good and cooperative working relations with trade union leaders like Ernest Bevin who became his Minister for Labour.

By his special efforts, Churchill became one of the very few Tory politicians who has ever gained the personal affection of union leaders.[7] They spent social time with him, they took him into their confidence on a number of occasions and made it clear throughout that he could count on their good will and even their cooperation if his rewards in terms of favourable policies would be 'reasonable'.[8]

Churchill capitalized on this experience in the postwar era when the Tories moved sharply to embrace the welfare state and the managed economy during the late 1940s. Once he returned to office as the first postwar Tory Prime Minister in 1951, he made it clear that he wanted peace and cooperative relations with the Trades Union Congress, whatever the price. His orders to his Labour Minister, Walter Monckton, followed this attitude specifically.[9] Monckton, in turn, carried them out to the letter.

Although there were grumblings from some of his colleagues that he was selling out to the unions, most of them were quite happy to go along. They were too mindful of the experience of the General Strike and of the new circumstances of interventionist government.

At the same time, the fundamental vulnerability of a Tory government was equally apparent. The basis of Churchill's approach was fear, fear that trade unionism would disrupt and otherwise undermine Conservative government which did not enjoy the close relationship which a Labour government could use as leverage in pressuring cooperation. Instead, Conservative government would need to 'buy' cooperation, if that was possible. If it was, it would likely pay an unacceptably high price as many thought Churchill had.

The Conservative experience in its relations with the TUC over the following two decades confirmed their worst fears.[10] Their need to manage the economy in order to meet the commitments of the economic and social contract of 1944 did make them very vulnerable to trade unionism. Churchill succeeded in keeping the good relations that he wanted, but he did so at the price of allowing inflationary pay increases which in turn fueled the series of economic crisis which his successors could not resolve. Time after time, Anthony Eden, Harold Macmillan and Sir Alec Douglas Home tried unsuccessfully to create effective producer group relations. Instead, the TUC made political capital out of its intransigence. And it did so without much fear that an angry and frustrated Conservative government would do much either to punish them or impose damaging policies. They knew that the Tories had so embraced the commitments of 1944 that they would never risk taking the electoral consequences of striking down the resulting collectivist process.

Change in this process did occur during the middle and late 1960s.[11] The economy slipped into an almost permanent state of crisis as militant trade unionists staged highly disruptive and often unofficial strikes as part of their effort to press the obvious advantage that full employment and economic security provided to them. As a consequence, both political parties began to consider the possibility of legislating 'good' industrial behaviour while retaining their commitments to the postwar pattern of economic management. Neither Labour nor Conservative politicians wanted to take the risk of a fight with the trade union movement, but on the other hand, they could no longer risk their electoral fortunes by continuing to fail to halt Britain's steep economic decline.

The Wilson Government and then the Heath Government tried in different ways to wrest the advantage from the Trades Union Congress.[12] The Wilson Government tried to legislate restraint on militant behaviour which would be sufficient to restore the authority of union leaders. The Tory Government led by Edward Heath started from a completely different view. The Tories accepted that they suffered an inherent disadvantage in any collectivist interaction with the TUC. Therefore, the Heath Government sought to develop a framework of law as well as an economic policy which would put that relationship on 'automatic pilot'. The law, enforced by the courts, would constrain industrial behaviour. Their economic policy simultaneously would operate without need of any *active* 'advice, cooperation or acquiescence' from the TUC.

Both approaches failed miserably between 1968 and 1974.[13] Their common weakness was that they were susceptible to union negative power, albeit veto power, which they were designed to reduce or end. Union power simply continued to flow from government's commitment to manage the economy to provide economic security and well-being, rather than from the institutional arrangements and rules which the political leadership attacked. Political leaders seem to have understood this problem from the beginning. But they felt constrained from changing the terms of economic commitment because they believed that the political bidding process in Britain continued to demand their fidelity to its terms and especially to full employment. The outcome of the attack and of the ferocious struggles between the unions and government thus clearly reconfirmed union power and even carried it to new heights.

But Heath's Conservative Government was a watershed in the history of collectivist politics. His defeat obscured the important point that he was the first Tory really to face up to the dilemma of their relationship with the Trades Union Congress and trade unionism. While he failed miserably, he took away from the TUC its secret pleasure at having a Tory government in office. He showed them that they no longer could expect that Conservative politicians would inevitably be paralyzed from taking policy initiatives or meting out policy punishments for their failure to 'behave' in accepting the government's conduct of economic policy. Nor could they expect any longer that a Tory administration would take them into the decision-making process no matter what role they played. To the contrary, Heath showed them that the Conservative Party wanted them out of the decision-making process and weakened from their long-standing position of being able to deliver vetoes and paralysis and stalemate against their policies.

These were his intentions from the beginning. That he failed to accomplish them directly tended to obscure their effect indirectly. But the truth is that he not only created a level of intimidation working against the TUC but he insured, by the degree of his own defeat, that succeeding Conservative leaders like Mrs Thatcher would certainly take up the challenge with even greater vigour. They would try to find new ways around the collectivist dilemma, while the TUC itself would suffer some of the fears that Conservatives felt in the wake of their own so-called victory in 1926.

(i) The Thatcher period

This point was not missed by Mrs Thatcher and her colleagues. They sharply criticized Mr Heath for his collectivist relations as part of their attack on his leadership. Later, they made the same issue and their own prescription for change a central part of their incumbency of office.

Their indictment of Mr Heath was that he did not use the political and institutional advantages he held.[14] They criticized his loss of nerve in making his famous U-turn in 1973 and for entering into fruitless and as it turned out suffocating talks with the TUC. They also criticized him for not having the guts to take advantage of the political leverage he held once he did get into a confrontation with the Miners in 1974.[15]

Mrs Thatcher made it clear that she intended to remedy Mr Heath's deficiencies.[16] She intended that her Conservative Government would carry out its economic responsibilities free from the debilitating influence of relations with organized labour. The collectivist shackles must be broken, she said, so that government could again operate to undertake policies which it thought best for the nation as a whole.

These views hit just the right chord during the spring of 1979.

An important element of the Conservative Party had long subscribed to an anti-collectivist position but it wasn't until the events of the 'winter of discontent' that the popularity of their views spread to the wider electorate. Mr Heath had initially taken a similar approach and enjoyed a similar popularity in the wake of 'In Place of Strife', but his own U-turn in 1973 followed by his confrontation with the Miners in 1974 had shattered faith in the possibility of ending collectivist politics without the most disastrous conflict. Mrs Thatcher was able to ride the crest of this new wave of anti-collectivist, 'let's do something about the unions' sentiment straight into office.

This was her advantage, but it was also her disadvantage. As Mr Heath did, Mrs Thatcher started from a public endorsement of anti-collectivism which gave her considerable political license to govern without nearly so extensive a process of consultation and bargaining as the predecessor Labour Government suffered. Moreover, she also had the advantage of public approval for legislation that would constrict union power.

Her disadvantages, however, were no less important. She started with bedrock support from that element of the Conservative Party which was anxious to correct the mistakes of the Heath Government. They wanted to get on with the job of doing something about union power which they condemned Heath for abandoning when the going got tough. They gave Mrs Thatcher considerable support in that effort. At the same time though, Mrs Thatcher faced a large and powerful element of the Tory Party which did not accept this approach. They continued to believe that Mr Heath unnecessarily provoked the union movement and put himself out of office by his stubbornness.[17] They strongly opposed what Mrs Thatcher wanted to do in these circumstances as another suicide confrontation that could only lead to serious damage to the nation as well as to the Party. Both views thus posed a danger to Mrs Thatcher. On the other hand, her supporters would allow no deviation from a hard line. On the other, her enemies, whom she was to dub the 'wets', would be looking for every opportunity to prove her wrong as well as unfit to continue to lead.

The mood of the wider electorate was somewhat different and a bit contradictory. Mrs Thatcher held a major advantage because the public continued to be disgusted by their memories of the previous winter. Support therefore remained strong for her intentions to dampen union power by restrictive legislation and to exclude union leaders from national decision-making processes. Yet, memories of 1974 and the 'three-day week' also remained salient and the public was therefore equally intolerant of even the hint of widespread disruptions, whether by the unions or well-intentioned political authorities waging their own counterattack.

Mrs Thatcher therefore had to recognize that there were limits beyond which she could not press. She could press aggressively for change, but only within a peaceful context. This was a difficult challenge because the union movement well understood that its own strength was best exercised in a conflictual and highly negative context.

2. THE UNIONS AT THE BEGINNING OF THE THATCHER GOVERNMENT

Whatever Mrs Thatcher's advantages and disadvantages, those of the union leadership were decidedly on the negative side. Intra-union politics, industrial relations and the state of the economy were all working to the movement's disadvantage.

Probably most worrisome was the situation within the union movement itself. This was a time of important leadership changes. Change, especially when it comes at moments of stress, is difficult for any organization. While change offers the benefit of new ideas and the potential for more flexible responses it also produces dislocation in the crucial relationships which affect decision-making and implementation. The union movement quite naturally enjoys both these advantages and suffers these disadvantages at times of leadership change. But in a number of ways the union movement finds these changes more difficult than most organizations, and this was especially true during the late seventies.

Leadership in a union and in a union movement is particularly crucial for success. This is the case for several reasons. First, a union and the entire movement are the collective expression of working people seeking security and improvements in their pay, conditions of employment and in the advantages which the society offers. Their leaders not only express and negotiate their demands but provide the crucial rallying point behind which the strength of the organization depends in great measure. Union officials are the only full-time workers whose main activity is to accomplish this rallying point and to carry the collective will into action and thereupon to fruition. Unless leadership does its job with considerable skill and charisma, unions are not only in danger of failing to win their goals but in danger of losing their existence.

This point applies also to an organization like the Trades Union Congress which is the spokesgroup for the collective of individual unions. It must, like individual unions, be able to enunciate goals and purposes in order both to rally support from its members and to interact successfully with the government of the day. Its success in doing both directly affects its viability as an organization.

The nature of these tasks tends to create highly personal leadership in the British union movement. Those who succeed to be leaders do so by combining considerable political skills with an enormous patience. They do not succeed by policy promises to the extent that their political counterparts do. Instead, they tend to gain support and position by the consistency of their loyalty to the general cause as well as by their personal rapport with colleagues and their attitudes toward the philosophic direction of trade unionism. Once at the top, they show enormous loyalty to the ideas that got them there, while at the same time they adopt stances which they hope will protect them from arguments and criticism that would undermine their positions.

Since this process produces highly stylized and personal leadership, change is not easily appreciated. Traditionally, succession has been slow and institutionalized, though quite smooth because each new leader could count on a high degree of loyalty during his incumbency and security of tenure until the retirement age of 65. However, this has been much less true since power has dispersed to the shop floor. Leaders now depend both for their selection as well as their continuing influence once in office on the consent of those they govern. They remain highly personal leaders but in a considerably more vulnerable situation. This makes the effect of change more uncertain and difficult.

The actual situation in 1979 was that particularly strong union leaders who had skilfully mastered the new conditions of leadership had retired. This collectivity was not only strong of intellect but had demonstrated their prowess and cemented their authority by winning great 'victories' over two prime ministers. They shared similar ideological views and used their professional camaraderie to forge a common front on which they could and did make decisions which were very effective within their own unions as well as within the TUC. More colloquially, they were a 'hard act to follow'.

Jack Jones, the leader of Britain's largest union, and Hugh Scanlon, leader of the second largest, are the most important examples of this process. Both came to power in the late sixties as champions of wage militancy and the power of shop stewards and local union organizations. As such, they gained inordinate influence with their weaker and more isolated colleagues on the General Council. Unofficial strikes, which were so rampant at the time, were not so threatening to their leadership. This advantage of being 'with' and often 'ahead' of their members coupled with the inherent advantage they held by their control of the TUC's largest unions endowed them with unprecedented influence within the General Council and with whatever government was in office.

The 'In Place of Strife' conflict and then the Heath years only added to their power and domination within the TUC. Working with other distinguished though more moderate leaders like Lord Allen and Lord Greene they won great victories which propelled them into Wilson's own Cabinet room for nearly non-stop consultation by 1975. No union leaders, not even those just after World War II, ever attained the influence on a moment-by-moment basis that these leaders did. It would therefore have been very difficult and perhaps impossible for any succeeding leaders to have achieved the position that Jack Jones, Hugh Scanlon and their colleagues occupied.

This problem of comparative weakness did indeed plague the new generation of leaders at the Transport Workers and the Engineers beginning in 1978. Moss Evans, for one, started with this as well other handicaps. First, Jack Jones had undermined the position of the Transport Worker General Secretary – whoever he would have been – by vigorously dispersing authority to the local union organizations. Control has always been a problem in so disparate a union as the Transport Workers, but it was much more so when Evans took office. Jones himself had dominated by the force of his powerful personality and especially by the loyalty he had created with those to whom he had given authority. He could not transfer that loyalty and command to his successor because it was so highly personal.

Evans was thus left to build his credibility in an organizational setting which was now dotted with strong and jealous independent power centres.[18] Some evidence of the trouble that Evans was to inherit had already appeared in the last days of Jones' incumbency when the great leader himself was rebuked by his own Conference on the question of wage restraint which Jones by then strongly supported.

This problem of wage restraint and the relationship between the TUC and the General Council was the second difficulty which Evans and others inherited. The gradual souring of union influence on the Callaghan Government had alienated a growing number of rank and file members. The 'winter of discontent' occurred largely because of this long slide and even the most prominent leaders like Jones and Scanlon saw their prestige erode for themselves and their successors. Furthermore, unfruitful TUC–Government cooperation had produced fissures within the General Council which the new leaders also inherited. This left them considerably more divided than their predecessors had been in the days of great struggle and victory when they had made their reputations.

The profile of the General Council which thus emerges at the time of the Tory victory is one of dissension and a lack of strong leadership, as well as pessimism about how to face the threat which they all agreed was menacing.

(i) The unfavourable economic context

The other major worry which trade union leaders faced in May 1979 was an unfavourable economic situation. Put succinctly, the Conservatives started with the perverse advantage that declining living standards coupled with relatively high and growing unemployment were sapping union strength. The concept of the 'lad around the corner waiting for a job'[19] was slowly creeping back into the union psyche for the first time in decades. The chaos produced by union militancy during the previous winter did not hide the hard truth that the labour market was depressed and in turn was contributing to the first decline in union membership in some years.[20]

This economic weakness also produced serious divisions within the TUC over the long-standing issue of wage restraint. Militants and moderates reopened their seemingly endless debate on new terms. This time it was the moderates who were most unhappy. They complained that the 'winter of discontent' again showed that attention by negotiators to the 'going rate' was self-destructive.[21] It produced unnecessary strikes and illusory settlements. Their argument at its sharpest was that inflationary wage increases not only dissipated quickly into higher prices but that they created serious political problems within the labour movement. High wage gains put union leadership into a more vulnerable and ultimately weaker position because of the unreasonable expectations they created. Leaders could not risk refusing their members' dreams for high wages even though fulfilling the demand was counterproductive and even unrealistic in the context of a weakening job market.

The new Government thus inherited a good strategic situation in terms of economic leverage with the Trades Union Congress.[22] Its predecessors had already abandoned much of the postwar economic commitments and the economic situation stripped away the rest. The TUC was left to argue within itself about how to recoup its strength while it had little power to influence actual government policy.

3. THATCHER VERSUS THE TUC: CONFLICT WITH A DIFFERENCE

The importance of the early days of the Thatcher Government were that they added impetus and solidified the direction in which the relationship between the union movement and government had already been moving. The Tories brought to office their own special attitudes and relationship with the union movement. These were added to the legacy of the 'winter of discontent' and four years of slipping union influence on a Labour Government which had embarked on a modified economic policy. The commitment to the economic and social contract of 1944 was already waning and with it the promise of full employment which directly underwrote the power of trade unionism and indirectly its place and influence in national decision-making.

The effect of these changes was the beginning of post-collectivist or anti-collectivist politics. For trade unionism, this meant not only less influence but a far more unpleasant economic context for its membership. It meant an era of high and rising unemployment along with a falling standard of living. It meant a recession and diminished prospects; declining trade union membership and a general disenchantment with a political process which was undermining its own legitimacy.

The key question produced by the Thatcher Government was whether these changes would be permanent. They represented, it was now certain, a powerful challenge to union power but could it be sustained? A positive answer certainly depended most heavily on the success of Chancellor Howe's monetarist economic policy. Economic well-being had been the most important issue in British politics for more than three decades. Government after government had lost office because it had failed to solve the problem within the context of Keynesian management of the economy. Now Mrs Thatcher was proceeding in a new direction, with its strong implications for union power. Her success or failure would probably answer the question about whether trade unionism would return to the fringes of power from which they had been called by Churchill's Coalition Government at the beginning of the Second World War.

The two main areas of interaction were to be the traditional ones of economic policy and industrial relations. These are quite naturally at the heart of the business which government and unions have with each other. Of the two, the economic was certainly the most important to both. The Government focused on this area especially because it was firmly committed to making radical changes which involved a complete and absolute break with the Keynesian tradition. Even though the Callaghan Government had already gone some distance in this direction, the Thatcher purpose was considerably more thorough and aggressive. Not only did it propose to reverse the tradition of high government intervention and spending, but it was also determined to change the rules of economic decision-making itself. By the terms of its plans, it would no longer need the high intensity of advice, acquiescence and cooperation which its predecessors had depended on trade unionists to deliver.

The first weeks of the Government's incumbency proved to be crucial because they created the pattern of interaction between both sides that prevailed for the following years. The interplay between industrial relations and economic policy was fascinating. Each side struggled during the early weeks to test the resources as well as the resolve of the other. The Thatcher Government, for its part, sought to take the initiative for its plans while learning how far it might go without provoking the sort of Heath-style conflict which it desperately wanted to avoid. The union movement, for its part, sought to overcome its own quite obvious weakness, confusion and damage from the 'winter of discontent'. It sought to convince the Government that it could and would inflict unacceptably damaging conflict if the Government pressed forward with its plans.

The Government had much the best of the struggle. It did what it wanted on economic policy. Although the TUC objected vehemently to its monetarist approach, it had neither the access, influence or ideas with which to mount much of a counteroffensive. Even in a personal exchange with the Prime Minister, it failed to make its arguments very effectively and suffered the humiliation of being on the short end of a lecture from her about the virtues of her philosophy. TUC leaders found themselves by the end of Mrs Thatcher's two months in office increasingly resigned to waiting passively for what they were sure would be her own self-destruction by the failure of her policies over time.[23] They knew there would be a terrible price to pay in terms of unemployment and a fall in the standard of living of their members but they were at a loss to know what to do about it. The situation was a mirror image of their own weakness and lack of purpose at that moment. It was as if a terrible natural weather disaster was approaching and even though they saw its potential, there was nothing they could do about it. They would organize rallies and protests and send out pamphlets, but they knew all of these would be no real antidote at all. Time would be the crucial factor and they would have to hope that it worked their way, because if it did not the era of their influence would certainly be at an end.

By contrast, trade unionists did not feel nearly so pessimistic about industrial relations. The Heath legacy together with the practical fear which Tories had of industrial disruption gave the union movement greater leverage in this area. The Tories started with a commitment to legislate and would certainly proceed to do so, but the TUC could count on having greater influence in this area. In fact, the prospect of dealing with James Prior, the new Employment Secretary, and the knowledge that Tories were susceptible to real influence was a kind of salve for their ineptness in the economic policy area.

This point was certainly not lost, however, on Mrs Thatcher and her colleagues. The course of the argument between the TUC and Government about industrial relations was thus interesting as it proceeded to the enactment of mildly restrictive legislation during the following spring. The TUC exercised genuine influence and a degree of intimidation, but at the same time the Tory leadership cleverly used this TUC advantage against other union interests. The Tories let the TUC enjoy satisfying influence in the industrial area and with James Prior as a kind of deflection against what might have been a more potent argument and even conflict over economic policy. The TUC had its way with James Prior to a great degree while it neither talked to nor influenced Sir Geoffrey Howe who proceeded, largely without pressure, to do what he wanted.

(i) Economic policy

No government ever proceeded to operate its economic policy in the postwar era with so little union influence on its terms and conduct. Sir Geoffrey Howe was able to start his term as Chancellor with the luxury of near isolation. He drafted and presented his Budget without meeting the TUC and without really considering its views.[24] He then proceeded to implement the terms of his budget with no more than a single meeting and almost no interaction with the TUC General Secretary or any of the members of the General Council. And the one meeting with the General Council, including the Prime Minister, proved to be a short farce which demonstrated the weakness of the TUC and only added further confirmation that he and his colleagues could proceed in their intentions as they wanted – even though the TUC itself was vehemently opposed both to his philosophical direction and to the details of his proposals.

The period from 4 May 1979, when Mrs Thatcher moved into Number 10 until 27 June when she met the General Council was thus quite a remarkable period of weeks from the point of view of economic policy-making. Looking back over the landscape of the post-World War II era it is impossible to find a time when an incoming government did not seek out, no less listen to, the attitudes of the Trades Union Congress.[25] Even the Heath Government, which gave a cold shoulder to the TUC about the construction of its industrial policies, sought the pro-forma advice of the TUC on economic affairs. Though it was like the Thatcher Government in its determination to have its own policies which would avoid entanglement with the union movement, it was careful to at least 'tip its hat' to the trade union movement, in an area which was considered part of its legitimate pressure group concerns.

The General Council and the General Secretary did try to get access, but they were coldly turned down with the lame excuse that the Chancellor would be too busy to see them until after he had presented his Budget.[26] Other efforts to exert some influence, to get their views considered, all went for naught. The best the TUC could do was to issue a statement pointing out that they continued to recommend an economic stewardship based on the proposals they made to the previous Government in their February Annual Economic Report.[27] Chancellor Healey had more or less ignored them at that time and it was certain that Chancellor Howe would do the same now.

The Chancellor therefore spoke to the House of Commons on 12 June from an unprecedentedly 'pure' position, stating the undiluted views and plans of his Government. They stood in stark contrast to the TUC, and set out for all to see the constrasts between both Keynesian and monetarist views of economic policy and consequently the contrasting interests of both trade union power and the general future of collectivist politics.

In his budget speech, the Chancellor broke with the past in his first words.[28] He spoke of Britain's decline compared to its European allies under economic policies which had clearly shown themselves to be bankrupt. It was precisely those ideas which the TUC counselled – though he did not refer to the unions explicitly – that he insisted had been so misguided and an utter failure. And the only area in which he agreed with Dennis Healey's approach was his stress on monetary performance particularly including the setting of money supply targets. Otherwise, Howe rejected Healey's 'notions of demand management', expanding public spending and his 'fine tuning of the economy'.[29]

The specifics of his Budget clarified the sharp disagreement. The economy's poor performance, he said, was not due to a shortage of demand. The failings were on the 'supply side' produced by the action and interventions of the Government itself, including laws that stifled enterprise and imposed punitive taxes.[30] He promised to break through those obstacles by reducing personal income tax burdens and shifting them to the Value Added Tax (VAT), as well as by reducing government expenditures and selling off shares in government-controlled enterprises.[31] The civil service staff would be reduced, support for local authority and nationalized industries would be cut, as would a host of government-sponsored industrial and regional development schemes.

From beginning to end the Chancellor stated views and proposals which were anathema to trade unionism. Howe blamed government interventions for the failures of economic performance, whereas the TUC put its full faith for an economic revival on government management of the economy.[32] The TUC urged more spending in the public sector as well as the strengthening of the commitment to support nationalized industries. The new Government promised just the opposite. The TUC emphasized the broadening of social welfare programmes; the new Government talked of economies. The Government put its faith on a renewal of private initiative while the TUC couldn't see how this would work except for the benefit it would bring to the few rich in the community. All in all, Congress House found nearly everything to be unhappy about.

The TUC Economic Committee met on the day after the Chancellor spoke.[33] It was indeed a sombre occasion. There was no shortage of unhappiness and bitterness. The atmosphere was somewhat reminiscent of the early Heath years except that Committee members seemed more pessimistic. One of the major contrasts with that earlier period was the mood of self-criticism and underlying dissension.[34] Everyone was agreed about the nature and seriousness of the Tory threat.[35] If there had been any illusions before, they had certainly been wiped away by the Chancellor's speech which seemed nothing less than a promise of attack on every fibre of union interest. Yet, there was in addition that gnawing feeling of helplessness coupled with the more terrible sense that they had somehow brought this all down on themselves by the events of the last year and the general acquiescence of the previous four.[36] They rued their inability to get control of events during the 'winter of discontent' at the same time that they rued their own docility for the years before that.

The staff view of the Chancellor's speech avoided these self-recriminations and focused instead on the more philosophical as well as practical implications of what the Government promised to do. Peter Jenkins' article in the *Guardian* that day very much hit the mark of their views.[37] Jenkins doubted the validity of the four 'articles of faith underlying the Chancellor's policy'. He wondered whether it was really true that letting people use more of what they earned does indeed have an incentive effect? He asked whether there really would be greater freedom of choice if the role of the state was reduced? He further asked whether reduced government borrowing, because of lower expenditures, would 'leave room' for a more vigorous private sector. And finally, he doubted whether those who negotiate for working people would come to know better the consequences of their behaviour. He reminded his readers that the 'catch-phrase of the Conservative fifties was "I'm alright Jack" '.

As did Jenkins, the Committee clearly answered these questions in the negative. 'We are entitled to wonder', Jenkins asked, '. . . whether there is such a thing as an austerity–incentive Budget or whether that is not a preposterous contradiction in terms'.[38] But could the Government survive the pressure for wage inflation, whatever its radical policy intentions? There were many on the Committee who doubted that they could stand fast for long – perhaps not even through the next winter, given the spurt of inflation which the rise in the VAT to 15 per cent would inevitably promote.[39]

The problem in practical terms for the Committee, however, was how to do more than wait and see what happened. How could they fight back? How could the TUC retain its influence against a determined government policy which was to snuff that influence out? Militants wanted to answer these questions with an all-out conflict, but the majority was considerably more timid. They would demand to see the Prime Minister, to wage a national campaign of protest, to issue detailed policy refutations but the majority including the General Secretary was very much against open warfare.

The Committee finally did get its meeting with the Prime Minister on 25 June. It learned then how dismal was the potential for its own influence, how far it had slipped in having real power in national economic decision-making and how lacking in its own sense of purpose.

What hurt more than anything about the Thatcher meeting was how thoroughly TUC leaders were humiliated by the Prime

Minister even though they had carefully prepared for the session.[40] The TUC staff had drawn up position papers on each issue, and in sum had produced a lengthy agenda which amounted to a kind of indictment of the Government's plans. The strategy was to allow Lord Allen, the Committee's chairman, and Len Murray to take full responsibility for the discussion.[41] Other members were to remain quiet in order to insure that Allen and Murray exercised the strongest possible leadership and especially to prevent the Prime Minister or any of her colleagues from attempting to exploit differences of agreement.

Nothing went as planned. It was a real disaster from the start and there was no hiding from the TUC's bankruptcy. From the moment they set foot into Number 10 they could not escape the contrast with their previous visits during Jim Callaghan's Government.[42] They had always met Callaghan in the Cabinet room.[43] Even during the years of declining influence and then during the 'winter of discontent' Callaghan had quite explicitly received them in that room which symbolized their special relationship. Now, Mrs Thatcher quite explicitly did the opposite. She, Sir Geoffrey Howe and James Prior together met them in another and considerably less pretentious room. The atmosphere was cold, stiff and formal. The smiles and handshakes were brief and forced.

There is no doubt that the TUC delegation was extremely intimidated by the atmosphere from the outset.[44] They had expected the coolness, but the stiffness and formality were surprising. In part, the earlier experiences of many of them during the Heath period cued them in the wrong direction. Those earlier meetings were not usually very fruitful but Tory ministers always had seemed to go out of their way to create at least a superficial friendliness. That was not the case this time and its effect was to expose the delegation's own sense of weakness and timidity.

Mrs Thatcher immediately converted this intimidation into an overwhelming advantage. She literally seized control of the session right at the outset.[45] The TUC's plans and strategies went out the window as she held the floor for virtually the entire hour the meeting lasted. Many of the TUC participants later said that the fact that she is a woman had an important effect.[46] They felt that their delegation as well as Mrs Thatcher's colleagues tended to be more deferential than they would have been to a man. They especially noticed that Howe and Prior were unusually quiet.

The TUC really never got to its agenda. Instead, they listened passively as the Prime Minister lectured to them like, as one union leader put it, a 'school marm'.[47] Others regarded her comments as little more than an election address, replete with a lesson in monetarist ideology. What rankled them most, though, was the Prime Minister's comments that she too was a public employee, and that she had received considerable electoral support from the trade unionists which they represented.[48] She insisted that this support demonstrated that their membership was beginning really to understand that high pay settlements would only provoke savagely higher unemployment.

These comments finally proved too much for some of the TUC participants who had promised to keep quiet. Moss Evans for one could not restrain himself any longer.[49] He broke the TUC's strategy by sharply telling the Prime Minister how much he resented her comments. There was no real follow-up debate, even though several TUC representatives got in brief comments. Before they knew it, though, she closed the meeting by inviting them back whenever they wanted to talk – though none of them believed that they would find anything to talk about. At any rate, she did not promise to listen.

Licking their wounds, they went back to Congress House to decide how to pick up the pieces of their disaster. They could see quite clearly that the Prime Minister recognized and relished their disarray.[50] She seemed absolutely delighted that she had given them hardly a minute's attention during the entire hour. She seemed even more delighted that she was able to needle them about the defections of their membership from the Labour Party during the election. In sum, she seemed to sense that she had the leverage in her hands and could do whatever she wanted. Nothing they had heard, therefore, dissuaded them from their earlier conclusions. Whether they liked it or not, the Government would go ahead with its economic policies while the TUC could, for its part, do little more than wait for those policies to fail.

The General Council accepted this view when it met the following day to hear the Economic Committee's report of the meeting and its consequent recommendations.[51] After a period of unanimous grumbling and fist-waving at the Government, the Council adopted a statement both criticizing the government's economic policies and initiating a campaign to sell what it called a 'positive alternative strategy'.[52] In truth, this strategy was a restatement of the proposals which the TUC had made repeatedly to the previous Government and in its 1979 Economic Report. It recommended nearly everything which the new Government opposed: 'a balanced growth of employment and output in both the public and private sector'; steps to block import penetration; a broad consensus about the distribution of income and wealth; an increased social wage; and the strengthening of publicly-owned industries.[53]

The TUC's official counterstrategy was to be a national campaign. Its terms and its approach strongly demonstrated how removed the TUC had become from significant debate with Government. Its leaders had no illusions that they would have much effect with the campaign. Defeat for the Government's policy would really need to be self-inflicted and on such a defeat hung the future power of the trade union movement.

(ii) Industrial relations policy

The Government's powerful determination to translate its 'ideology' into a radically new economic policy coupled with the TUC's own sense of its weakness and impotence to oppose that determination deflected significant interaction between both sides to industrial policy. This deflection somewhat perversely suited the purposes of each to a tee.

The Government did start from a strong and genuine commitment to legislate new restrictions on industrial behaviour. The events of the 'winter of discontent' including its own prescriptive statements during those months produced the political requirement that it 'do something about the unions'. At the same time, however, the 'something' was couched in gentle and consensual terms which explicitly avoided any commitment which might provoke a new Heath-style confrontation. This meant that there would inevitably be interaction about industrial relations but also that the Government wanted to keep that interaction at a relatively low temperature.

This formula suited the Government for other reasons, and more surprisingly the TUC as well. The advantage for the Government was that interaction on industrial relations at this level would provide an important political access point as well as method of interaction which would have been otherwise foreclosed by the threatening nature of its economic approach. Whatever their public statements and personal feelings about collectivism, senior Conservative leaders even on the Thatcher sides of things recognized that it would be impossible to immediately cut off collectivist relations. Heath had, in the main, tried to do just that during the early seventies and as a consequence catalysed the TUC's still considerable negative power during the months of distance and cold war. This new Government profited by this lesson by understanding that it needed to keep channels of communication open to the TUC and the member unions in order to defuse the build-up of a potentially serious challenge. Its economic policies needed breathing space, and while it moved to adopt industrial commitments that it had made in terms of legislation it could use that forum to maintain some semblance of contact and appearance of reasonableness.

For its part, the TUC was happy to accept the government-initiated deflection of relations to the industrial because in its difficult position it was glad to have an access point and happy to find an avenue through it could exercise some degree of influence. This was necessary for its own internal well-being and credibility with its membership. It was also necessary because it dearly wanted to avoid the isolation which the Government's economic policy threatened to impose. Whatever the public view of the Heath period, the facts were that the TUC never wished to be isolated during those early years and panicked during the later period when it feared that its lack of influence during the Miners' crisis would provoke a real economic disaster for its membership.[54] The General Council had always come down on the side of maintaining relations with whatever party was in power, and it was equally anxious this time to maximize its relations wherever it could, however threatening the Government might seem.

(2) James Prior as ambassador to the TUC

It was for these reasons that James Prior as Employment Minister became a kind of ambassador to the TUC. His position as it evolved was quite unique. Because of his personal relations with trade unionists, his role as a senior Tory, as a member of the Cabinet, and most importantly as an adversary of Mrs Thatcher, Prior gained credibility in a multi-faceted role. Both sides found him infuriating at times, but in the main recognized that he was the only person who could coordinate, communicate and bargain between them.

Prior had been the opposition spokesman on employment before the election but trade unionists were still genuinely surprised that Mrs Thatcher actually appointed him to that position once she had won office.[55] They reasoned that the new Prime Minister found him much too soft and consensual to suffer his presence at so crucial a ministry as Employment. Flushed as she was with a large majority, they expected her to name a Thatcherite hardliner as Minister for Employment and then to have him press ahead with much more aggressive legislation than the Conservative Manifesto had promised.

Prior's selection was therefore a surprise and a pleasant surprise at that, although there was some scepticism about what Mrs Thatcher might be up to. Most optimistically, they hoped that Prior's selection signalled a so-far undetected softness in Mrs Thatcher's views about industrial relations or at least her acknowledgment that the softer view of moderate Conservatives needed to be given significant attention.[56]

They could not, however, help but wonder about the interplay between the new Prime Minister and Jim Prior. During the run-up to the election, Prior had consistently and quite carefully discounted and buffered the draconian suggestions which Mrs Thatcher and her colleagues hurled at the most inflammatory moments.[57] Prior even went so far on several occasions as to telephone individual TUC leaders to apologize privately for statements made by his less temperate colleagues.[58] He genuinely seemed to remember the lessons of the Heath period in a way which made him want to proceed cautiously in union-government relations. He also seemed to believe that consultations and good personal relations would be far more fruitful than either the aloofness or icy hostility which other Tories practiced.

These soothing images about Prior did not reduce, however, the curiosity and argument within the trade union movement about what role he would really play and why he was in the Cabinet in the first place. There was wide understanding that Prior and Thatcher did not get along personally and that they disagreed about a great number of theoretical and policy issues. At first glance then it appeared he had been included in the Cabinet simply because he was a senior Tory politician who by

British practice was entitled to a senior role in the new government. But something else seemed to be involved. After all, Mrs Thatcher had appointed him to the very sensitive position of Minister of Employment. He would therefore be responsible for relations with the union movement which one might have thought she would want to entrust to a closer ally. And following the same train of thought, it was important to remember that Prior's careful manoeuverings, statements and behaviour toward trade union leaders over several previous months did give the impression that he was following some sort of designed strategy.

A school of thought developed at the TUC which speculated that Prior and Thatcher were embarking on a Mutt-and-Jeff approach to trade union relations.[60] The strategy, if in fact there was one, was that Thatcher would speak to the wider electorate about trade unionism in harder terms. She would continue to insist that government should restrain union power and expel it from the centre of national decision-making. The Tories would gain by this approach in national terms because it fit so well with her own personal views and dovetailed with public opinion which was unhappily tending toward anger about union behaviour. At the same time, Prior could speak from his own more cautious and 'soft' inclinations both to the trade union leadership and to worried Conservatives. The contradiction of this approach might create some awkward situations but in general would deal with a problem that itself was contradictory. Trade unionists would be advantageously off-balance, while the general public would see and hear views which both satisfied their get-tough attitude and salved their deep-seated fear of conflict that might produce a return to the crisis atmosphere of the Heath period.

Trade union leaders were divided in their opinion of this view. But they were agreed at least that they needed to remember that Prior is a Tory and that he is a member of a Cabinet generally opposed to union interests.

The first days of the Government's incumbency did nothing to dispel this confusion. Contradictory comments by Prior and Thatcher continued and, as it turned out, set the pattern for the Government's behaviour in the coming months and years. For example, Prior made it clear that there would be legislation on picketing, the closed shop and financial aid for ballots. But he indicated that the Government at that time was not thinking of going beyond these limited measures. Mrs Thatcher, by contrast, wavered between seconding his predictions and promising to consider and possibly take up harsher measures. At the same time, Prior launched into an effort to convince trade unionists that he was really a 'good fellow' looking out for their interests and a person who stood between themselves and the return of great confrontation. He approached trade unionists on his own, asking them for social occasions which was not very typical of his Tory predecessors.[61] He also went out of his way to generate sympathy for his position: he indicated – and he did this repeatedly – how surprised he was even to be holding office and how really lonely he was in the midst of so many tough Thatcherites.[62] His closest assistants and advisors spread this same message wherever they could.[63] They also took every opportunity to send this message to the media, which dutifully reported it in every story. In fact, a pattern of journalism developed in which this Mutt–Jeff approach became the benchmark for reporting Mr Prior's activities.

Thatcher–Prior sparring over industrial relations thus became a key and ongoing enterprise. There is no question that the issues were important and that the differences were genuine. There also seems little question that the Conservative leadership was none too unhappy to exploit the situation to its own advantage *vis-à-vis* both the union movement and elements within the Conservative Party. But more importantly, it also became apparent that industrial relations occupied a different role from the one it had under Mr Heath. It was not nearly so important to the purpose of the Thatcher Government. Rather, it was a politically sensitive and explosive policy area which was to be 'managed' and 'exploited' where possible. Mrs Thatcher and her Chancellor, Sir Geoffrey Howe, did have a great interest in reforming industrial relations. They had always believed that the Industrial Relations Act had been a good and proper way of dealing with the problem. But the experiences of that time and especially the public rejection of that approach made another undertaking of that magnitude impossible at the moment.

(b) Deflection in action

Industrial relations policy-making was first off the mark, as Prior began consultations with the TUC almost immediately. The early meetings in May and June followed a predictable but important path. Taking his cues directly from the Conservative Manifesto, Prior talked generally about his plan with a wide variety of union officials.[64] He met with Murray and Ken Graham, as well as the TUC Employment Policy and Organization Committee.[65] The contacts were frequent and lengthy, quite opposite to those the Chancellor did *not* have. Throughout, Prior encouraged extensive dialogue while continuing to insist that it was politically necessary to proceed with legislation on the three prime areas of strike ballots, the closed shop and picketing.

The Heath precedent. The contrast in this process with that which the Heath Government followed was striking and politically beneficial to Prior's interests. Robert Carr, who was Heath's first Employment Minister, had orders to construct a comprehensive industrial relations bill. But he also had orders to avoid consultations about the bill that involved any discussions about the underlying principles of the proposed legislation.[66] Talks with the TUC about details were fair game but the Prime Minister refused to permit the TUC into areas which he regarded as the prerogatives of elected political authorities.[67]

The truth was that Heath believed that he held a political mandate which licensed him to avoid such consultations.[68] And for Heath this situation was particularly advantageous because the experience of previous Tory and Labour governments demonstrated to him that consultations on the principles of proposed legislation would lead to its emasculation. It was only later in his term, after bruising struggles with the unions, that Heath reversed himself and actually championed pluralist contacts. But in 1970, Heath was intent on altering the pattern of producer group politics. He quite directly intended to avoid the paralysis of his policy and by doing so create a new pattern of industrial relations which would operate without the union movement's persistent, intimidating influence.[69]

Robert Carr implemented these views with an overzealous and destructive fidelity. He refused to meet with the General Council until he had published his proposals although his work was not ready until four months after the Tories took office. Then, once he did meet with senior union leaders in mid-October 1970 he started by telling his guests that he would not negotiate about the eight central 'pillars' on which his *Consultative Document* was based.[70] They were welcome to discuss the details of his recommendations but talks would have to be completed within a period of only one month.

Carr's attitude infuriated union leaders who were well primed for a fight anyway.[71] They had spent the week before the meeting with Carr studying the proposals which, from their point of view, contained just about every disagreeable idea they could imagine. No amount of telephoning, letters or private conversations by the General Secretary, Victor Feather, budged Carr an inch. The actual meeting therefore seemed only to confirm for union leaders that the Government was determined to directly attack their fundamental influence. They quickly became convinced that they were in for an all-out fight and since the Government wasn't serious in wanting real consultations, they wouldn't waste their time any further. In fact, they abruptly stalked out of the meeting with Carr and went back to Congress House to plan their campaign against the Government's proposals.[72] In doing so, they also unprecedentedly broke relations with the Government and precipitated a silence in communications which lasted for about 18 months.

The ensuing struggle ultimately demonstrated that the Heath Government was so intent about legislating a new pattern of industrial relations that it set itself up to fall victim to that very power. Nothing Carr could have done would have better galvanized union resistance. His legislative proposal was clearly a provocation. It is therefore likely that the TUC would have resisted it with great strength for substantive reasons, but not with quite the unanimous zeal which they did in the wake of Carr's affront.

Union leaders had long enjoyed the unifying influence which the Tory bogeyman provided. Carr and Heath played the bogeyman role to a tee, which ultimately caused the leadership to perceive a very positive gain for an all-out fight whatever the result.

The Government's behaviour at that time was particularly fortuitous for the TUC's interests because of the background of intra-union relations during the 1960s. The growth of the shop steward movement had undermined the power of central union leaderships and, with it, at least some of the authority of the TUC itself. The Wilson Government, in fact, had tried to bolster this sagging authority by its 'In Place of Strife' proposal. Mrs Castle at that time believed that the chances for peaceful industrial relations and producer group politics were much brighter when union leaders could speak with effectiveness. Thus the presence of a belligerent, threatening Tory administration was welcome because it provided a badly needed catalyst for centralized union leaders to recapture their strength.

The TUC thus became a real tiger rather than the paper tiger which Heathites dipsaragingly labelled it at the beginning of the Government's term. Its weaknesses melted away as it rose to the challenge. The TUC did become for that period an organization with determined and coherent though negative strength which was quite ready and capable of fighting back.

(c) The argument in 1979

In 1979, Jim Prior proceeded very carefully to avoid any such catalyst from developing.[73] Industrial relations were not on the centre stage; economic policy was more important this time. His purpose and the strategic situation was thus quite different from those Robert Carr had faced. He needed to legislate, but much less comprehensively. He also needed to avoid conflict with the unions, which Carr had not so much feared. But he also was charged with managing his responsibilities so as to focus union attention and interaction toward himself and thus away from economic argument.

The main issue in the first weeks was more about timing than about substance. The Cabinet was split over the question of how far legislation should go toward imposing legal discipline on trade unionism but there was at least agreement that the first round should be limited.[74] Timing was a different matter. Prior wanted to proceed very cautiously while the Prime Minister took the position that the electorate had provided a clear mandate for immediate action.[75] Mrs Thatcher worried that this mandate was an opportunity that had to be seized before it dissipated in the fire of controversy which would certainly develop over her aggressive budget initiatives.

The first contacts between the unions and the Government in May and June tended to reinforce Prior's go-slow tactics. Caution is certainly the best way to describe the Government's approach at least through the middle of June. Although trade unionists themselves seemed to be cautious, their persistent references to 1973–4 helped to keep ministers susceptible to Prior's urgings.

And the angry response which Howe's budget produced only added to this view. By 18 June, Ministers were in fact leaking to the press the decision by Mrs Thatcher to hold back the publication of a consultative document for industrial relations until after the TUC Congress in September.[76] These reports emphasized that ministers did not want to provoke a row leading to the development of a powerful anti-Government campaign. They especially wanted to prevent upcoming union conferences leading to the TUC Congress from holding full-scale debates on industrial policy.

Everything changed, however, after Mrs Thatcher met with senior TUC leaders on 25 June. The Prime Minister and Sir Geoffrey Howe were 'amazed' by that session.[77] Union leaders seemed surprisingly docile and confused and lacking in consensus about how to deal with them. Having lived through the Heath debacle, they had expected to find the unionists a 'tough lot'. Instead, they were surprised at how easily Mrs Thatcher dominated the meeting and even at moments when she did not, how poorly union leaders presented and persisted in their case. The breakdown of discipline at the end of the session when a number of unionists 'dropped in' their comments confirmed their disarray.

Confident now that she had the situation under control, the Prime Minister pressed her own wish to publish the consultative document immediately.[78] Jim Prior, who was also at the meeting, did not resist with nearly as much intensity as he had earlier. He was surprised himself by the ineptness of the TUC team.[79] Also, his own soundings revealed that the TUC was fairly well reconciled to the limited legislation which the Manifesto proposed.

It is interesting to note how intensively Prior canvassed the attitudes of Trade unionists during this period. He showed how sensitive he and his colleagues were to union attitudes. Both he and his assistants made a great number of phone calls and personal contacts before and after the TUC meeting with the Prime Minister.[80] Senior trade unionists were surprised by this velocity of contacts and only later realized that the Employment Minister was 'testing the water' for a dramatic change in timing.[81]

New leaks to the press at the beginning of July heralded the change in strategy. Keith Harper, in a particularly frank and informed article, candidly described the Government's new thinking.[82] He reported that the TUC's muted reaction to the budget indicated to ministers that there was no reason to hesitate in moving forward with consultations leading to legislation. Harper did not mention the impact of the Thatcher–TUC meeting nor of Prior's soundings, but his point was the same: the Government had decided there was not so much to fear as they had thought. They had also, very importantly, decided to use the apparent advantage of Jim Prior's personal position in the relationship.

One week later, on 9 July 1979, the Employment Department published the working papers.[83] These followed the Conservative Manifesto quite closely. At the same time, Prior and his assistants were careful to let Len Murray and the press know that some sections were open to negotiations.[84] There were also suggestions that if the TUC would acquiesce in the Government's positions on picketing and the closed shop – which were easily the most contentious – that the Government would not go ahead with plans to make unions liable for social security benefits paid to strikers. Prior also hinted to Murray and other unionists in private that union cooperation with these proposals might well forestall additional legislation for which Prior said that other Conservatives were already pressing.[85]

Formal union reaction to the working papers followed a predictable pattern.[86] Union leaders lined up to tell the press how angered they were by the proposals. Not only were the specific proposals a challenge to good industrial relations, they said, but they charged that the whole package was only the first step in a much broader attack on trade union power. They envisioned that the Government would proceed bit by bit toward the kind of framework which the Industrial Relations Act had attempted to impose.

What was missing from these public complaints, though, was the threat or even the hint that the union movement was thinking of a new all-out war. This was a key omission which was predictive, it turned out, of the history of the passage of the Employment Bill over the following months. That scenario proved to be more interesting for the struggle it produced within the Conservative Party than for the argument it generated between the Government and the TUC. It was testimony to the weakness of the movement and to its obvious relief at the mildness of the legislation.

Over the weeks and months that followed the TUC did wage an extensive public campaign against the legislation, but its efforts were no more than uninspired. The details have been extensively reported elsewhere.[87] What was really important about this period was not these public activities but rather the TUC's more covert efforts to influence the course of intra-Cabinet and intra-Conservative politics. The TUC specifically wanted to make sure that hardline Tories did not capture the initiative for their harsher proposals.

Congress House thus went out of its way to acquiesce in a complicated strategy which bolstered Jim Prior's position. For example, Len Murray and his colleagues loudly and repeatedly emphasized how threatened the movement would be by the terms of the existing bill. Their complaints were genuine but their vehemence served two other political purposes. It fulfilled their quite natural interest in using threatening Conservative policies in a traditional effort to rally union support for their own and the TUC's leadership. And just as importantly, it served their interests in helping Jim Prior to convince his Conservative doubters and adversaries that they could in good conscience support his proposed legislation because it really would administer the kind of restrictive medicine against union power which they wanted.

The main responsibility for developing and coordinating this strategy with Jim Prior fell to Harry Urwin, the chairman of the TUC's Employment and Organization Committee. Urwin was perfect for the job. He had not only been a chief negotiator during the 'winter of discontent' but he also enjoyed the best personal relations with Jim Prior of any member of the TUC leadership. Prior and Urwin had known each other for a long time and Urwin had been a key liaison to Prior during the days before the election.

Urwin's formal responsibilities were to negotiate with Prior about possible changes in the proposed legislation. The more covert and political manoeuverings were woven into this primary task. So beginning in the early fall of 1979, Urwin and Prior were in contact quite frequently and during some periods as often as every day.

It proved to be a carefully orchestrated scenario.[88] Urwin needed to project the public image of the angry and tough TUC bargainer, insisting on changes where trade unionism believed its fundamental rights were under attack. Prior also needed to project the image of a tough and resistant advocate who was determined to have his legislation and not to retreat very far from the 'reasonable' and 'limited' proposals which he had set out.

The two of them worked together with unusual effectiveness given the long history of unfruitful Conservative–union relations.[89] Of course, their purposes were quite limited and largely defensive so the situation was unique. But each could take satisfaction that the outcome was as mutually satisfying as could have been expected. Prior, for his part, did succeed in winning the TUC's acquiescence to the bulk of his proposals, as well as its acquiescence and sometimes active participation in a strategy to outflank his Tory critics. Urwin, for his part, succeeded in getting Prior to drop what he and his colleagues believed were the most 'obnoxious' provisions.

Each side thus came away from the interaction relatively satisfied that they had done as well as they could have in the circumstances. The TUC took considerable solace from the mildness of the final legislation as well as the ultimate victory which they helped Prior to win over his Cabinet adversaries including apparently the Prime Minister herself.[90] They hoped that by this work they had developed a useful and influential access point to this Government which a few months earlier seemed totally immune to their views.

4. CONCLUSION

TUC satisfaction at the skill of its defensive cooperation with Jim Prior could not obscure the uniquely weak and vulnerable position it suffered at the beginning of the Thatcher Government. In nearly every way trade unionists were being reminded about how much their influence had slipped during the last half decade, and how bleak the prospects were for its recovery in this new era of economic management.

The despair TUC leaders had felt at the Conservative victory in May 1979 was thus well founded. They had been right in projecting that Mrs Thatcher would make good on her anti-collectivist promises and also that she stood an excellent chance of success in that purpose. In some ways, they had even underestimated their position. The ease with which Sir Geoffrey Howe proceeded to construct and then implement an economic policy which so thoroughly disagreed with their views and attacked fundamental union interests was almost shocking. It would have been literally unimaginable a decade earlier or even five years earlier for a British government to openly and successfully press policies which directly undermined the 'sacred' notion of full employment and a constantly rising standard of living. Sir Geoffrey in a few short weeks had thus stripped away the economic foundations which the Trades Union Congress had assumed were inviolable for more than three decades. And when the most senior TUC leaders went to protest these policies to the Prime Minister herself they were forced to suffer the indignity of a schoolboy's lecture against which they hardly uttered an important peep.

What limited success they had against the industrial relations legislation hardly measured up to their economic defeat. Jim Prior's proposals were not very threatening and the TUC's success in working with him to defeat hardline Tories was a small victory indeed compared to the process of shaping a new economic direction for Britain which was taking place elsewhere.

In sum, therefore, the beginning of the Thatcher Government offered a disturbing preview for trade unionists of their relationship with a Conservative government in the post-Keynesian era. While it was true that Mrs Thatcher came to office with the advantage of political license to move aggresively against the unions, the hard reality of their diminished influence in larger terms could not be ignored. It was now very unlikely that the traditional pattern of union vetoes against helpless and fearful Conservative governments would soon reappear except if the policies of those governments went so badly that the weakness was self-inflicted.

5 Post-collectivist Politics: a Modest Proposal for Strengthening the Trades Union Congress

The major theme of this study has been the weakness and therefore the ineffectiveness of the Trades Union Congress. Britain's economic condition as well as the purposes of trade unionism itself have been among its casualties. So too has the collectivist political process which unions themselves promoted in order to win their place at the centre of national decision-making.

Events at the beginning of the Thatcher Government as well as throughout the 'winter of discontent' are valuable examples of union–government relations at the beginning of an emerging post-collectivist era. They provide the basis for speculating about how relations are likely to develop during the rest of this decade. Even more interesting, though, they provide the basis for speculating about how trade unions might finally agree to strengthen the TUC and thereby end its costly impotence.

1. LESSONS FOR POST-COLLECTIVIST POLITICS

(i) The Callaghan Labour Government and the 'Winter of Discontent'

The fact that a Labour government was the first to abandon Keynesian economics and the 1944 economic and social contract demonstrated how thoroughly collectivist politics had failed. After all, it was a Labour government which had pioneered the new group politics and was most susceptible to union pressure that it be faithful to its wartime commitments. Moreover, Labour's policy change in 1976 was highly risky because it threatened to provoke confrontation between both sides of the labour movement at a time when unions still seemed to be riding the crest of their 'victory' over Edward Heath only eighteen months before. Yet, the Government did make its move because ministers could see no way that the Trades Union Congress or the larger trade union movement could or would cooperate *sufficiently* to solve Britain's overwhelming economic problems.

The resulting post-Keynesian policies which included strict control of the money supply and of government spending kicked away the support from much of the power which trade unionism had used in demanding and winning its place in national economic decision-making. This change created a new and unexpected problem for the Trades Union Congress. Although its weakness had contributed to the demise of collectivist politics and an end to Keynesian economic management, the new era ironically produced even greater demands for its effectiveness from the Labour Government and its member unions. But without benefit of the leverage which full employment had formerly provided, the Trades Union Congress found itself even weaker, more divided and therefore certainly unable to satisfy these demands.

The consequence of this dilemma was that decision-making within the TUC came under debilitating stress. At its best and when dealing with routine matters, the TUC's decision-making process has always worked carefully to finesse its problem of inherent weakness compared to its individual union members. This has been accomplished with the cooperation of union leaders who have been willing to accept a high concentration of authority at Congress House in order to maximize the organization's bargaining ability. Junior leaders thus defer to their senior colleagues, thereby allowing a reasonable degree of effectiveness to be created. This tactic has worked well on a day-to-day basis within a limited context. Since 1976, however, the stressful circumstances of the Government's new economic policies have made even the more routine decision-making difficult and important decision-making sometimes nearly impossible. This development was seen most vividly during the fall of 1978 when the General Council failed on a tie vote for the first time to endorse a vital agreement which its senior leaders had worked out after considerable struggle with the Callaghan Government. This defeating tie-vote in the Council testified to the centripetal stress which post-Keynesian policies were imposing and are likely to impose in a post-collectivist era.

The agreement which the Council defeated represented an effort to save the Labour Government in a way which the TUC would never have done for a Tory government. The fact that three months later, in February of 1979, the General Council approved a second agreement for the same purpose showed that the old ties between the union movement and its political wing are still somewhat viable. But the rebellion within the Council stands as a more significant event because it was so completely unprecedented for General Council members to reject the proposals of their own colleagues on such an important and even vital matter. This behaviour showed quite clearly how much the vaunted negative power of trade unionism has turned inward and against its already weak potential for collective action.

(ii) The beginning of the Thatcher Government

The early days and months of the Thatcher Government proved to be even more jarring for unionists than the chaotic events of the 'winter of discontent'. Union leaders were depressed from the beginning because they knew that industrial disruptions had contributed importantly to Mrs Thatcher's election as Prime Minister. Moreover, they knew that she came to office eager to exclude them from national politics which would even more harshly attack the basis of their power. What was worse, though, was that they sadly expected that she would succeed in these purposes where her predecessor Tory Prime Minister, Edward Heath, had failed miserably.

The course of events during May and June of 1979 and throughout the balance of that year showed how right they were in their pessimistic musings. Mrs Thatcher and her colleagues showed in the conduct of their industrial and economic policies that the traditional advantage which unions had enjoyed against Conservative governments had disappeared. Now that unemployment was sapping union power and government had begun to manage the economy without so much need of union cooperation, Tory politicians no long worried so much about bidding for union cooperation or at least acquiescence to its policies.

The potential for a permanently changed situation was thus fully in place. Tory governments especially can now hope to gain the advantage by the same distance and hostility from trade unionists which had formerly worked to their disadvantage. And even Labour governments or perhaps Social Democratic–Liberal governments can expect that the weakening pressures of post-Keynesian economic policies will lower the price they will have to pay for cooperation which the trade union movement may well be eager to deliver.

2. POST-COLLECTIVIST POLITICS IN BRITAIN

(i) The politics of full employment and unemployment

These two episodes help to sketch out the likely form of politics in a post-collectivist Britain. The loss of full employment and then the rise of high unemployment have obviously been the key factors undermining union power and thus changing the face of the political process. Political leaders have not been surprised that change has occurred but they have been surprised by the speed, intensity and nature of that change.

British elite including political and union leaders have long been sensitive to the potential consequences of unemployment. The all-party undertaking in 1944 to guarantee full employment as official policy expressed this sensitivity. There was no unanimous agreement about what constituted politically unacceptable levels of unemployment, but the figure of 500,000 was most commonly mentioned. The great surprise of the last five years for these leaders therefore has been how little political reaction they encountered as the numbers of unemployed rose first to a million, then to a million and a half and then well beyond. No one has dared to suggest that this number could be carried out endlessly but it has become clear that the political tolerance point was much higher than anyone could have imagined.

The importance of this revelation for union–government relationships is that political leaders discovered that they could 'live with' a level of unemployment which was high enough to seriously damage the power of their union adversaries. Here then was the key to waging the successful counter attack against union power which political leaders had tried to undertake with disastrous results at the end of the 1960s and early 1970s. Thus, it is very likely that politicians will tenaciously hold on to this new potent weapon even while praising the merits of full employment in their election manifestos.

(ii) The politics of government's continued management of the economy

The factor which will most likely enhance countervailing union power against the effects of permanently higher unemployment will be government's continued management of the economy. Although politicians have learned that they can 'live with' much higher rates of unemployment than they expected, they have also learned that the quality of their management of the economy is still as politically sensitive an issue as it had been all during the collectivist years.

The Thatcher Government has certainly demonstrated this point convincingly. Both its plans and its experiences reveal how difficult it would be for a British government to begin to dismantle the managed economy, and how unlikely a British government is to want to undertake the task.

A close reading of the 1979 Conservative Manifesto reveals that even the Thatcherites understood before they took office that much of the consensus which led to the 1944 economic and social contract and later to Churchill's fulfilment of these commitments in office still runs deep in the body politic. The 1979 Manifesto promises a new stress on private initiative, the removal of government intrusion, lower government expenditures, the elimination of government jobs, and government divestiture of some of its holdings. But its brave words are sprinkled with considerable timidity and its specific proposals no more than limited at best.

The actual conduct of the Thatcher Government in office has not been much bolder. Its economic policies departed strikingly from the past and their effect has been obvious. But more of government's management, control and operation over the economy has stayed the same than has changed. It is not only very difficult to dismantle so vast and complex a structure, but the Thatcher Government has not been anxious to lose control of the mechanism which strongly affects its political fortunes. For example, it has been far more willing to provide subsidies and rescues for important firms threatened with bankruptcy than its Manifesto would ever have promised.

The experience of the last few years therefore indicates that it is very likely that practical political considerations will force governments of both parties to continue most of the elements of their management of the economy. Thus, they are also going to need and want to interact as cooperatively and effectively as possible with trade unionism which, after all, still holds the keys to the delivery of a productive labour force.

The sum of this discussion, then, is that the course of recent events suggests that unions and government will continue to find their relationship a matter of prime importance. What is likely to be most different in this new era is the advantage which government will hold because of the continuing presence of high unemployment. Unions will want and need the Trades Union Congress to more effectively defend and promote their interests which are very likely to be under severe pressure. Thus, its constituent members may finally decide that they will have to find a way to make the sacrifices necessary to overcome the TUC's destructive weakness.

3. CREATING AN EFFECTIVE TUC:
A MODEST PROPOSAL

British trade unions have been searching for a way out of their predicament for years, but without notable success. The problem has been that each proposal for change has involved structural and rule changes which would have increased power for the TUC at the expense of individual unions. These ideas inevitably stirred intransigent jealousies which worked to obstruct reform in every particular. It is clear from these many experiences that any approach which is to have a decent chance for success must involve subtle, indirect and long-term changes which do not stimulate the usual overpowering negative reactions from member unions.

The orginal Citrine–Bevin strategy for enhancing TUC power had considerable merit because it recognized the necessity for just such an approach. The General Strike had killed any chance that unions would soon again explicitly entrust great power to a trade union centre, though the need for a strong directing authority for labour was obvious. The Citrine–Bevin idea was for the TUC gradually to win such power indirectly. They therefore pressed for the development of strong interventionist government from whom they intended to win access and influence. By doing so, they expected that they would greatly expand the areas in which member unions would look to the TUC for leadership and therefore authority.

Citrine and Bevin were certainly right about the effect that government management of the economy would produce. The TUC *was* drawn from the fringes of power into the centre of national decision-making thus giving birth to the era of collectivist politics at the end of the Second World War. The miscalculation in their thinking, however, proved to be that constituent unions responded to this development by contributing shares of their authority to a trade union centre *much more slowly* than Citrine and Bevin had anticipated. Collectivist politics thus failed to work in relation to the speed at which government took control of the economy and made consequent demands for union participation in bargaining and implementing economic and industrial policies. By the late sixties, the gap between government 'demand' and TUC 'delivery' had widened to a politically unacceptable degree.

A modest proposal

The beginning of the post-collectivist era would seem to be a good time for trade unionism to make another effort to strengthen the TUC into an effective pressure group. The 'winter of discontent' and the beginning of the Thatcher Government certainly offer enough evidence to suggest that individual unions are going to want the protection of a strong TUC more than ever. This should provide enough incentive to stimulate serious consideration of real change. However, even such circumstances will be unlikely by themselves to cause unions to agree to structural and rule changes which they vehemently have opposed for so many years. The answer will still need to come in a more indirect, subtle and long-term way.

One possibility which would take this approach is the development over time of a much closer *intra-union* 'political' relationship. This would especially involve the participation of union leaders more directly and continuously in the business of the TUC. At the present time, *no* leaders of individual unions are full-time officials of the TUC. There is no reason why this must be the case. The inclusion of union officials on the full-time staff and in the leadership of Congress House might well produce a new and very beneficial pattern of decision-making and interaction.

This idea is not completely new. It has been considered and *rejected* by the General Council, though *only* as a limited proposal to name a union leader instead of a TUC civil servant as General Secretary. In fact, when Len Murray was elected to be General Secretary in 1973 there was brief and inconclusive thought given to the election instead of a person of Jack Jones' stature.[1] But there was little taste for the idea.

The most cogent arguments against the idea have been that the appointment of a strong union figure would provoke jealous dissension while the appointment of a weaker, less controversial leader would do nothing to strengthen the TUC while ensuring the incumbency of a General Secretary who would not even know how to use the expertise of his civil service. The advantage of the present system, its supporters argue, is that the General Secretary can impartially muster the best possible support from disparate elements in the union movement while enjoying the informed collaboration of a staff whom he has known and worked with for years.

This kind of argument has been focused, of course, on the narrow question of who shall be the General Secretary but the same points would have undoubtedly been made if consideration had been given to wide leader participation at the TUC. *What union leaders have failed to appreciate, however, are the potent disadvantages they suffer by strictly separating themselves from the work of the TUC.* They do not know nearly so much as they would about the business of national trade unionism! They do not know each other or the possibilities which their relationships might produce as well as they could! They do not understand many of the possibilities and limits of interaction with government or between their own unions! And they cannot serve as effectively as they might in linking the national union centre with local union officials and the rank and file. The quality of such a relationship is highly important to the viability of a strong directing authority at the top.

Looking just at the position of General Secretary, it is possible to imagine some major gains from the incumbency of a union leader. Probably the most important of these would be the addition of the 'political' talents that a union leader could bring to what is clearly a very 'political' job. Union leaders have learned and honed their political skills as a necessary requirement for a successful career in their individual unions. In many ways, they need to operate as politicians do in a different context. Bidding for office is a way of life which includes demonstrating a keen sense of democratic responsiveness and responsibility. Consummate bargaining skills, very good interpersonal relations and a feeling for building consensus are all part of their necessary credentials. Although the job description for the TUC General Secretary is different than for the General Secretary of any individual union, these political skills are indispensable.

The problem for the TUC until now has been that their General Secretaries have usually been intelligent, knowledgeable and very capable administrators who have had less developed political skills. This shortcoming is not surprising because career development at the TUC does not put as great a premium on political attributes. The job of department secretaries, which all General Secretaries once held, does involve careful political work with committee members as well as government ministers and civil servants. But it lacks the broad, public, high-powered political activities which union leaders perform and the TUC General Secretary must be able to display if he is to be very effective.

The career of Victor Feather as General Secretary ironically provides good evidence supporting this argument in favour of a union leader in his position. Feather, of course, was *not* a union leader himself but rather a TUC civil servant. His talents and attitudes and behaviour were much more like those of his union leader colleagues on the General Council than his predecessors or successor as General Secretary, each of whom was promoted from within the TUC government.

Feather was really a skilled politician who loved to negotiate, to fix deals and to socialize with other unionists. He was certainly no intellectual as Woodock and Murray were and are, but he had and applied talents which were more appropriate to the practical needs of the TUC. His adept negotiations during the 'In Place of Strife' controversy as well as his dealings with Edward Heath proved his talents. Heath, in fact, has frequently asserted that

Feather's retirement contributed to the Miner's confrontation because he was the only union official whom Heath felt he could negotiate with in good faith.[2]

Feather thus gained a special currency with his colleagues on the General Council. He was appreciated for his uncommon ability to negotiate with ministers, but he was most valued by his colleagues because they viewed him as 'one of them'. Whereas Woodcock and to a lesser degree Tewson and Murray have been regarded as somewhat distant, Feather was regarded wholeheartedly as part of their community. It was this special relationship which Feather was able to use in order to weave together the strongest and most effective General Council in TUC history.

The incumbency of a similarly talented and well-placed union leader as General Secretary would promise the same sort of gains for the TUC. It is conceivable, of course, that another Feather might emerge from within the TUC staff itself. But the chances are poor because the pattern of succession and the requirements for advancement within Congress House tend to produce bureaucratic rather than politically inclined candidates. It would be far more likely that a union leader who could be specifically chosen for these talents would be able to succeed in the way that Feather did.

The primary task of such a union leader would be to create a new sense of community between the centre and periphery of the trade union movement. Individual unions have too often used the strict separation between themselves and the TUC for their own narrow advantages. They have put distance between themselves and the TUC in order to use the national union centre as a scapegoat for whatever unpleasant developments they wished to deflect. This tactic has continuously undermined TUC credibility and therefore its potential as a directing authority. However, with a union leader as General Secretary and perhaps other union leaders similarly participating in subordinate roles at Congress House on a full-time basis, it would be considerably more difficult for individual unions to separate themselves from the business of national trade unionism. They would have their own leaders and colleagues in the front lines and their successes and failures would be part of the movement's own record.

The essence of this modest proposal is therefore that the union movement would best serve its interests by creating real political *interdependence* between individual unions and *their* Trades Union Congress. The British trade union movement must increase the level of personal interaction, intercommunication and the sense of responsibility for what happens at Congress House. This should be possible to accomplish. It does not involve any changes in rules or frontal assaults on individual union power. What it involves is the use of the leadership selection process in a different but already authorized way. The election of a union leader as General Secretary could occur on the retirement of Len Murray. The selection of other union leaders to serve as Deputy and Assistant Secretaries as well as Department Heads could be implemented over time, starting with the most important and sensitive positions. Gradually, in the Citrine–Bevin tradition, the TUC could work to fuse the movement together so that the TUC could effectively meet the challenge which the post-collectivist era will certainly pose.

Postscript

The premise that Britain has entered a new era of post-collectivism seems even more valid in mid-1982, three years after Mrs Thatcher took office. Individual union leaders talk of conflict and confrontation but whether they lead another 'winter of discontent' or not their harsh words cannot hide the depression which their movement now suffers. For much as the events of the late seventies and early eighties portended, post-collectivism is posing a dangerous challenge to union power.

The signs of trouble for the union movement are everywhere. High unemployment has become a seemingly permanent fact of life. Three million are currently out of work, including more than one million who have been without jobs for at least a year. TUC membership has already declined by nearly one million and is falling more rapidly than at any time since the depression. Union leadership both inside and outside the TUC continues to be weak and divided, and to be excluded from access to an influence with government. And the Tories keep proceeding with step-by-step legislation which seeks to restrain union behaviour.

Faced with all these problems, trade unionism should certainly recognize that there is incentive enough for its leaders to take up the task of reforming its strategies, tactics and structure, including consideration for the proposals outlined above. The major question which proceeds from this analysis in mid-1982 is whether these incentives are actually working to foster change. Will trade unionism respond to this challenge and rise above its traditional inhibitions to create a strong and directing Trades Union Congress?

The answers to these questions are only now in the making, but there are signs that the subject of reform is at least on the agenda. How far reform will proceed will be determined in all likelihood by how threatened constituent unions feel. Len Murray has always shared with his predecessors as General Secretary the conviction

136

that the TUC will become more powerful depending on how much its constituent unions need protection from policies which government is bringing or threatening to bring to bear against them. Using the yardstick in this new era of post-collectivism, it would seem that the prospects are at least brighter than usual.

The argument about reform at the TUC at this time pits two broad, informal groupings against each other. One group includes leaders who are generally from the largest unions and who are more militant or 'left'. The other group includes leaders who are generally from the medium-sized and smaller unions and are moderate or 'right' in their views.

The first or more militant group believes that the current depressed circumstances are transitory and intimately bound up with the incumbency of the present Tory government. Its leaders are much more willing than others to conflict and confront. They expect that their aggressive use of industrial action will win both larger pay packets and greater influence by forcing government to recognize union power and drop its present attack. For this reason, militants throughout the movement can join with the leaders of the TUC's largest unions in resisting efforts to tamper with the current distribution of power between their own individual unions and the TUC as a collective. They view the possibility of a much stronger TUC with considerable distaste because they are sure that an effective directing centre would force them to restrain their own aggressiveness. The larger unions such as the Transport Workers not only are in sympathy with the militant philosophy and general distrust of TUC authority but fear that a strong TUC would jeapordize their own current dominance in TUC decision-making.

Opposition to these militant but structurally status quo views come from more moderate and 'right-wing' leaders, many of whom lead medium-sized white collar unions. They argue that post-collectivism is a significant challenge transcending the Thatcher Government. They argue further that conflict has done no better than produce the political counterattack leading to the present difficult circumstances. The challenge for them therefore is to redefine union strategy in order that it win back union influence on government and its policy making process. Reform, especially the development of a stronger and more authoritative TUC, are vital so that trade unionism can go forward with an effective negotiating capability. In sum, the TUC need to lead the movement back 'to the table' and once there to enjoy the power to speak for and operate the collectivist participation which has now slipped away.

This sort of argument between militants and moderates, between the 'left' and 'right' is a very old one within British trade unionism. The difference in recent days is that the argument has focused more sharply on the question of the distribution of power within the TUC. The circumstances of these difficult times has predictably raised the temperature of the debate. How the TUC does its job of defending the interests of its member unions logically becomes a much more important topic.

The most significant event in this debate indicating that the force of reform is indeed stirring at the TUC took place at the September 1981 TUC Congress. Moderates pressed their long-familiar proposal that seats on the General Council be redistributed to provide places for all unions with memberships of 100,000 or more. This idea would clearly broaden the participation of union leadership in the General Council while striking at the dominance of both the larger unions and the 'left' majority – since many of the leaders who are now excluded are moderates. Just as in previous years stretching back for a long time, the General Council led by its largest unions objected to such change. But to the surprised delight of its supporters, the motion carried and the General Council was 'instructed' to plan for this change over the following twelve months.

The majority for this proposal was only very slight, but the decision was momentous nevertheless. Congress had voted for significant reform! The exact fate of this change, however, was not as certain as it seemed because the Transport Workers and other unions on the presently constituted Council could and are objecting to the details of the plan.

These events demonstrate that post-collectivism *is* working to force the union movement to consider the reform of its TUC. At the same time, the old jealousies, self-interests, and traditional divisions are continuing to obstruct change. The modest proposals offered in this study for gradually and indirectly strengthening the TUC by developing an interdependence between constituent unions and their central spokesgroup still seems to offer a sensible approach which might resolve this dilemma.

Notes and References

CHAPTER 1: THE PROBLEM OF TRADE UNION PURPOSE

1. Professor Samuel Beer first offered his theory of collectivist politics in *Modern British Politics* (Faber, 1965).
2. See several excellent books including: Leo Panitch, *Social Democracy and Industrial Militancy* (Cambridge University Press, 1976); Michael Moran, *The Politics of Industrial Relations* (Macmillan, 1977); and T. C. May, *Trade Unions and Pressure Group Politics* (Saxon House, 1975). Also see Gerald A. Dorfman, *Wage Politics in Britain, 1945 – 1967* (Iowa State University Press, 1973, and Charles Knight, 1974); and Gerald A. Dorfman, *Government Versus Trade Unionism in British Politics Since 1968* (Macmillan and Hoover Institution Press, both 1979).
3. The most concise and coherent statement of trade union purpose was made by the Trades Union Congress in its evidence before the Royal Commission on Trades Unions and Employers' Associations in 1966. While cautioning that no individual union or unionist might find this list completely satisfactory, the TUC nevertheless insisted that all of the following objectives enjoyed wide support as necessary to the 'good life, which is the ultimate objective of all of them':

   a. improved terms of employment
   b. improved physical environment at work
   c. full employment and national prosperity
   d. security of employment and income
   e. improved social security
   f. fair shares in national income and wealth
   g. industrial democracy
   h. a voice in government
   i. improved public and social services
   j. public control and planning of industry.

4. Data on wages, prices, employment and the other elements of Britain's economic performance can be found in Central Statistical Office, *Economic Trends* (HMSO, monthly).
5. Ibid.
6. For an excellent concise historical account of this period, see John Lovell and B. C. Roberts, *A Short History of the T.U.C.* (Macmillan, 1968) chaps 4, 5.

7. David E. Butler and Jennie Freeman, *British Political Facts 1900–1967* (Macmillan, 1968).
8. Lovell and Roberts, *A Short History of the T.U.C.*, p. 12.
9. Alan Bullock, *The Life and Times of Ernest Bevin* (Heinemann, 1960) p. 108.
10. TUC, *Annual Report 1920.*
11. Lovell and Roberts, *A Short History of the T.U.C.*, chap. 5.
12. Ibid., p.84
13. Ibid.
14. Also see TUC, *Annual Report 1924*, pp. 111–2.
15. Lovell and Roberts, *A Short History of the T.U.C.*, p. 84.
16. TUC, *The General Council of the Trades Union Congress*, 1924, p. 8
17. See Alan Bullock, *The Life and Times of Ernest Bevin*, 1960, pp. 279–371; and W. H. Crook, *The General Strike* (University of North Carolina Press, 1931).
18. Lord Citrine (Walter Citrine), *Men and Work* (Hutchinson, 1964) p. 238.
19. See my two earlier studies, Dorfman, *Wage Politics in Britain, 1945–1967;* and Gerald A. Dorfman, *Government Versus Trade Unionism in British Politics Since 1968* (Macmillan, 1979).
20. Ibid.
21. Interview with David Lea, 10 July 1969.
22. Interview with George Woodcock, 17 July 1969.
23. Interview with James Mortimer, 5 August 1969.
24. Dorfman, *Government Versus Trade Unionism in British Politics Since 1968,* chap. 2.
25. Ibid., chap. 3.
26. Interview with Maurice Macmillan, 16 August 1977.
27. For example, the Bow Group held a conference entitled 'Trade Unions in Britain: Paper Tigers or Threats to Democracy?' at Oxford University in November 1974.

CHAPTER 2: DECISION-MAKING STRUCTURES AT THE TRADES UNION CONGRESS

1. I learned a great deal about the General Council, including its hierarchical relationships and interactions with the TUC staff, by interviewing the following present and former members: Lord Allen, David Basnett, Frank Chapple, Frank Cousins, Lord Douglas, Moss Evans, Lord Geddes, Lord Greene, Tom Jackson, Ron Smith, Harry Urwin, Sidney Weighell and Lord Williamson.
2. For a brief description of the organizational structure of the TUC, see TUC, *ABC of the TUC,* latest revised edition.
3. The 'gold-plated six' became a popular TUC term during the early seventies at a time when this senior group represented the TUC in bargaining with Edward Heath.
4. This list and others that follow were extracted from various TUC *Annual Reports.*
5. The abbreviations stand for the following groups:
    E   Economic Committee
    GP   Finance and General Purposes Committee
    I   International Committee

6. The number of years that General Council members have served can be found at the end of each year's *Annual Report*. The figures here were calculated from TUC, *Annual Report 1979*, p. 715.
7. Interview with Moss Evans, 22 June 1979.
8. This comment and those which follow were collected during the interview I listed above. I must report that the General Council members I spoke with individually were nearly unanimous about these perceptions of the Council's behaviour.
9. I have reached the following perceptions about the role of the TUC General Secretary from information I gained in all of my TUC interviews, but especially from my interviews with the last four TUC General Secretaries: Len Murray, Lord Feather, George Woodcock and Vincent Tewson. George Woodcock, in particular, generously gave me a very great amount of his time.
10. See my argument in Chapter 5 that a union leader should be elected as the next General Secretary.
11. Interview with Lord Greene, 24 July 1969.
12. Interview with Len Murray, 31 July 1969.
13. Interview with Lord Greene, 4 August 1972.
14. Murray Interview. Also see the following articles about Murray: *World Times*, 2 August 1979; *The Times*, 2 August 1977; *Guardian*, 26 April 1977; *Guardian*, 26 January 1974; *The Sunday Times*, 2 September 1973; and *Financial Times*, 10 September 1973.
15. Interview with Vincent Tewson, 11 August 1969.
16. Murray Interview.
17. Ibid.
18. This comment and those which immediately follow were made in unattributable interviews with the TUC staff and General Council members during the summer of 1980.
19. Ibid.
20. Unattributable interview with a member of the TUC staff.
21. Interview with Edward Heath, 13 April 1978.
22. Ibid. I have heard these same comments from several sources, including Conservative and union leaders.
23. *Financial Times*, 10 September 1973.
24. Ibid.
25. Interview with Tom Jackson, 15 June 1979.
26. Interview with Lord Douglass, 15 July 1969.
27. Lord Greene interview, 4 July 1972.
28. Lord Feather interview, 26 August 1972.
29. Lord Greene interview, 4 July 1972.
30. Ibid., 31 July 1973.
31. My comments in this section are the result of four separate interviews with George Woodcock on 12 July 1969, 26 July 1972, 21 August 1972 and 26 July 1973. The first interview was held at the Commission for Industrial Relations just after he had become its Chairman. The last three interviews were at his home when he was retired.
32. Ibid.
33. Ibid.

34. Ibid.
35. Woodcock also greatly frustrated his subordinates on the TUC staff by his rejection of practical politics. They greatly admired his brilliance but his failure to act on his ideas and unwillingness to twist any arms at all made them feel quite impotent. Unattributable interview with very senior TUC official.
36. Woodcock interview, 12 July 1969. Also see George Woodcock, *The Trade Union Movement in Government* (Leicester University Press, 1968).
37. Woodcock interview, 12 July 1969.
38. This comment and others about Lord George Brown are attributable to an interview with Fred Jones, 14 July 1969 and with Sir Eric Roll, 14 July 1969.
39. Woodcock interview, 12 July 1969.
40. Ibid.
41. Interview with Jim Mortimer, 5 August 1969.
42. Woodcock interview, 12 July 1969.
43. See Gerald A. Dorfman, *Wage Politics in Britain 1945–1967* (Iowa State University Press, 1973) chap. 7.
44. Eric Silver, transcript of interview with Lord Feather, pp. 33–6.
45. Woodcock interview, 26 July 1972.
46. Eric Silver, *Victor Feather* (Gollancz, 1973).
47. Woodcock interview, 26 July 1972.
48. Lord Feather interview, 26 August 1969.
49. Silver, *Victor Feather*, pp. 146–7; and Dorfman, *Government Versus Trade Unionism in British Politics Since 1968*, pp. 36–7.
50. Heath interview.
51. This discussion is based on a great number of unattributable interviews with TUC civil servants from 1969 through 1980.
52. Ibid.
53. Ibid.
54. Ibid.

CHAPTER 3: THE POLITICS OF FAILURE: THE 'WINTER OF DISCONTENT' 1978–9

1. Current data on unemployment can be found in Central Statistical Office, *Economic Trends* (HMSO, monthly).
2. Interview with Lord Allen, 27 June 1979.
3. For details of that agreement, see TUC, *Annual Report 1977*, pp. 226–9.
4. For a discussion of that argument, see TUC, *Annual Report 1978*, Section G.
5. Ibid., p. 289. Also unattributable interview with a member of the General Council.
6. Interview with Frank Chapple, 29 June 1979.
7. *Winning the Battle Against Inflation* (HMSO, July 1978).
8. Unattributable interview with a member of TUC staff.
9. Ibid.
10. Ibid.
11. Ibid.

12. Interview with Tom Jackson, 15 June 1979.
13. TUC, 'Pay Policy After July 31', July 1978.
14. Ibid.
15. Ibid.
16. Unattributable interview with senior union leader.
17. *The Times,* 6 September 1978.
18. *Guardian,* 6 September 1978.
19. Unattributable interview with senior union leader.
20. *The Times,* 2 September 1978.
21. Unattributable interview with senior union leader.
22. Ibid.
23. Ibid.
24. Interview with Moss Evans, 22 June 1979. Also see *The Times,* 2 October 1978.
25. *The Times,* 3 October 1978.
26. *The Times,* 4 October 1978.
27. Ibid.
28. Evans interview, 22 June 1979.
29. Ibid.
30. My interviews over the last dozen years have consistently revealed a much greater degree of TUC staff agreement with Labour Government assessments of economic policy needs than TUC statements or policy stances otherwise indicate.
31. See especially *The Times,* 11, 12, 18 October 1978.
32. *The Times,* 26 October 1978.
33. Ibid.
34. Ibid.
35. *The Times,* 15 November 1978.
36. *The Times,* 16 November 1978.
37. Ibid.
38. Ibid. Mr Jackson made this point even more forcefully in my interview with him on 15 June 1979.
39. Ibid.
40. *The Times,* 15 November 1978.
41. For a full discussion of the 1973–4 Miners' Crisis, see Gerald A. Dorfman, *Government Versus Trade Unionism in British Politics Since 1968* (Macmillan, 1979) chap. 3.
42. Interview with David Basnett, 22 June 1979.
43. Ibid.
44. Unattributable interviews with two senior TUC staff members.
45. Ibid.
46. Ibid.
47. Ibid.
48. *Guardian,* 12 January 1979. Also, Evans interview, 22 June 1979.
49. Ibid.
50. Ibid.
51. Ibid.
52. *Guardian,* 12 January 1979.
53. Ibid.

54. Interview with Lord Allen, 27 June 1979.
55. TUC, *A Cause for Concern,* 1979.
56. Ibid., p. 25.
57. For example, *Guardian,* 18 January 1979.
58. Lord Allen interview, 27 June 1979.
59. *Guardian,* 17 January 1979.
60. Ibid.
61. Ibid.
62. Evans interview, 22 June 1979.
63. Lord Allen interview, 27 June 1979.
64. *Guardian,* 19 January 1979. Also, Evans interview, 22 June 1979.
65. Unattributable interview with a member of the TUC staff.
66. Evans interview, 22 June 1979.
67. Ibid.
68. *Guardian,* 19 January 1979.
69. Chapple interview.
70. Basnett interview, 22 June 1979.
71. Ibid.
72. Lord Allen interview, 27 June 1979.
73. *Guardian,* 29 January 1979, 1 February 1979.
74. *Guardian,* 29 January 1979, 1 February 1979.
75. Unattributable interviews with members of the TUC staff.
76. Ibid.
77. Lord Allen interview, 22 June 1979.
78. Ibid.
79. Ibid.
80. Ibid.
81. *TUC, the Economy, the Government and Trade Union Responsibilities – Joint Statement by the TUC and the Government,* February 1978.
82. *Guardian,* 15 February 1979.
83. *Guardian,* 5 March 1979.

CHAPTER 4: THE POLITICS OF CONTINUING FAILURE: THE
BEGINNING OF THE THATCHER GOVERNMENT, 1979–80.

1. Unattributable interviews with members of the TUC staff.
2. Interview with D. H. Urwin, 2 August 1977.
3. Interviews with James Mortimer, 1 August 1972, and with George Woodcock, 26 July 1973.
4. See Gerald A. Dorfman, *Wage Politics in Britain 1945–1967* (Iowa State University Press, 1973) chaps 5, 6, 8.
5. Ibid.
6. Interviews with Selwyn Lloyd, 5 August 1969; Aubrey Jones, 5 August 1969; Maurice Macmillan, 16 August 1977.
7. Joint interview with Lord Geddes and Lord Williamson, 2 July 1969.
8. Ibid.
9. 'Winston's riding orders to me were that the Labour Party had foretold grave industrial troubles if the Conservatives were elected, and he looked to

me to do my best to preserve industrial peace.' Lord Birkenhead, *Walter Monckton* (Weidenfeld and Nicolson, 1969) p. 276.

10. See Gerald A. Dorfman, *Wage Politics in Britain 1945–1967,* chaps 5, 6; and Gerald A. Dorfman, Government Versus Trade Unionism in British Politics Since 1968 (Macmillan, 1979) chap. 3.
11. Dorfman, *Government Versus Trade Unionism in British Politics Since 1968,* chaps 2, 3.
12. Ibid.
13. Ibid.
14. Several interviews with Peter Lilley, 1974–7.
15. Ibid.
16. Mrs Thatcher has expressed these views on scores of occasions. Hugh Stephenson has collected them in a good analysis of her first year in office. Hugh Stephenson, *Mrs Thatcher's First Year* (Jill Wormans Ltd., 1980) pp. 10–28, 62–77. Also see the comments of her close confidant Sir Keith Joseph, *Solving the Union Problem Is the Key to Britain's Recovery* (Centre for Policy Studies, 1979).
17. Macmillan interview.
18. Interview with Moss Evans, 22 June 1979.
19. Lord Williamson interview.
20. Lord Allen interview, 27 June 1979, and interview with John Thane, 23 June 1980.
21. Interview with Sidney Weighell, 7 June 1979.
22. Lord Allen interview, 27 June 1979.
23. This point was made repeatedly by *every* union official I interviewed in 1979.
24. Lord Allen was Chairman of the TUC Economic Committee and expressed great anger and frustration at Sir Geoffrey's studied isolation from TUC representations during this period. Lord Allen interview, 27 June 1979.
25. Ibid.
26. Ibid.
27. *Guardian,* 10 May 1979; and see TUC, *Economic Review,* 1980. Also see 'Thatcher Tells the Unions', *Guardian,* 23 May 1979.
28. *Guardian,* 13 June 1979.
29. Ibid.
30. Ibid.
31. Ibid.
32. For best statement of contrasting TUC views, see TUC, *Economic Review,* 1980.
33. *Guardian,* 14 June 1980; TUC, *Annual Report 1979,* p. 280; and Lord Allen interview, 27 June 1979.
34. Unattributable interview with senior union leader.
35. Ibid.
36. Ibid.
37. *Guardian,* 13 June 1979.
38. Ibid.
39. Interview with David Basnett, 22 June 1979.
40. Lord Allen interview, 22 June 1979.
41. Ibid.
42. Ibid.

43. Ibid.
44. Unattributable interview with a union leader who was present at the meeting.
45. Ibid.
46. I interviewed both TUC staff and union officials who were at this meeting. Most of them told me that their comments were not to be attributed.
47. Interview with Frank Chapple, 29 June 1979.
48. Lord Allen interview, 27 June 1979.
49. Moss Evans interview, 8 July 1980.
50. Lord Allen interview, 27 June 1979.
51. *Guardian,* 28 June 1979.
52. Ibid.
53. See TUC, *Economic Report,* 1979. Also see TUC General Council, 'The Economic Policy of the Government', 27 June 1979.
54. Dorfman, *Government Versus Trade Unionism in British Politics Since 1968,* p. 98.
55. Interview with Tom Jackson, 15 June 1979.
56. Ibid.
57. *Guardian,* 1 May 1979.
58. Unattributable interview with senior member of TUC staff.
59. Most union leaders took this point of view, but others – a minority – very much distrusted Prior.
60. TUC staff members most strongly embraced this view. Also Lord Allen's comments in *Guardian,* 1 May 1979.
61. Jackson interview, 15 June 1979.
62. Ibid.
63. Interview with Robert Shephard, 25 June 1979.
65. Ibid.
66. Interview with Alan Brown, 21 July 1972.
67. Interview with Edward Heath, 13 April 1978.
68. Ibid.
69. Ibid.
70. *Financial Times,* 14 October 1970. Also, interview with Lord Greene, 4 August 1972. Industrial Relations Bill, *Consultative Document* (Department of Employment, 1970).
71. Lord Greene interview, 4 August 1972, and Lord Allen interview, 16 November 1975.
72. Ibid.
73. Robert Shephard interview.
74. Unattributable interview with prominent Conservative who had access to Cabinet discussions.
75. Ibid.
76. *Guardian,* 19 June 1979.
77. Unattributable interview with prominent Conservative who had access to Cabinet discussions.
78. Ibid.
79. Ibid.
80. Robert Shephard interview.
81. Unattributable interview with member of TUC staff.
82. *Guardian,* 3 July 1979.

83. For a good summary, see *Guardian,* 10 July 1979.

84. Robert Shephard interview.

85. Unattributable interview with a member of the TUC staff.

86. See two TUC publications, TUC, *TUC Commentary on the Employment Bill,* 1979; and TUC, *The TUC Against the Employment Bill,* 1980. Also see TUC, *Annual Report 1979,* pp. 33–4.

87. There was an enormous amount of newspaper coverage of their story for about nine months from June 1979.

88. Unattributable interview with a member of the TUC staff.

89. Ibid.

90. Ibid. However, not everyone was happy with the outcome at Congress House.

CHAPTER 5: POST-COLLECTIVIST . POLITICS: A MODEST PROPOSAL FOR STRENGTHENING THE TRADES UNION CONGRESS

1. Interview with David Basnett, 22 July 1980.

2. Interview with Edward Heath, 13 April 1978.

Personal Interviews

Abbott, Janet, former Assistant to Alan Swindon, Director, Industrial Relations, Confederation of British Industry, 13 August 1975.

Allen, Lord, General Secretary, Union of Shop, Distributive, and Allied Workers; Chairman, TUC Economic Committee; member, TUC General Council: 22 July 1969, 16 November 1975, 10 August 1977, 27 June 1979.

Basnett, David, General Secretary, National Union of General and Municipal Workers; Chairman, TUC Economic Committee; member, TUC General Council: 22 June 1979, 22 July 1980.

Bendelow, Martin, Centre for Policy Studies, 22 July 1977.

Brittan, Samuel, Principal Economic Commentator, *Financial Times,* 20 June 1979, 28 June 1979.

Brown, Alan, Assistant Secretary, Department of Employment, 21 July 1972.

Brown, Judy, Head, Research Department, Amalgamated Union of Engineering Workers, 17 July 1980.

Butler, Michael, Assistant Under-Secretary in charge of European Community Affairs, 24 July 1975.

Carlton, Ann, Political Adviser, Ministry of Agriculture, 15 August 1977.

Castle, Barbara, former Secretary for Employment and Prices, 27 July 1972, 13–15 April 1978.

Chapple, Frank, General Secretary, Electrical, Electronic, Telecommunication and Plumbing Union; member, TUC General Council: 29 June 1979.

Coldrick, Peter, Secretary, European Trade Union Confederation, 29 July 1979 (by phone).

Cousins, Frank, General Secretary, Transport and General Workers Union; member, TUC General Council: 5 August 1969.

Derx, Donald, Deputy Secretary, Department of Employment, July, 1977.

Donovan, Lord (Terence Norbert), retired Chairman of the Royal Commission on Trade Unions and Employers' Associations, 1967–8, 21 July 1969.

Evans, A. M., General Secretary, Transport and General Workers' Union, 22 June 1979, 8 July 1980.

Feather, Lord, General Secretary, TUC, 26 August 1969.

Foggon, George, Overseas Labour Adviser, Foreign and Commonwealth Office, 2 August 1975.

Gray, Hugh, Member of Parliament, 8 July 1969.

Greene, Lord, former General Secretary, National Union of Railwaymen; Chairman, TUC Economic Committee; member, TUC General Council: 24 July 1969, 4 August 1972, 31 July 1973.

Hartley, Andrew, Deputy Director, EEC Office (London), 23 July 1975. 9

148

August 1977, 12 August 1977, etc.

Haggan, D. E., Deputy Secretary, National Industrial Relations Court, 3 August 1972.

Heath, Edward, former Prime Minister, 13 April 1978.

Hurst, Harry, Deputy Overseas Labour Adviser, Foreign and Commonwealth Office, 12 August 1975.

Jackson, Thomas, General Secretary, Union of Post Office Workers; Chairman, TUC International Committee; member, TUC General Council: 15 June 1979, 15 July 1980.

Jacques, Peter, Secretary, TUC Social Insurance and Industrial Welfare Department, 17 July 1980.

Lea, David, Staff Member, TUC Economic Department, 10 July 1969 (now Assistant General Secretary of TUC).

Lilley, Peter, Chairman, Bow Group; Investment Analyst, several interviews, 1974–80

Lloyd, Michael, European Communities Office (London), 20 July 1977, 25 June 1979.

Lowry, Patrick, Director, Industrial Relations, British Leyland, 8 August 1972.

Mackintosh, John P., Member of Parliament, November 1974, 20 July 1975, etc.

Macmillan, Maurice, former Minister of Labour, 16 August 1977.

Moore, A. B., Assistant Secretary, Department of Employment, 29 July 1975.

Mortimer, James, Chairman, Advisory and Conciliation Service; former member, National Board for Prices and Incomes: 5 August 1969, 1 August 1972, 19 July 1977.

Murray, Len, then Secretary, TUC Economic Department; now General Secretary, TUC: 31 July 1969.

Pendlebury, Rupert, Research Department, Amalgamated Union of Engineering Workers, 28 July 1972.

Pinder, John, Director, Political and Economic Planning, 28 July 1975.

Prentice, Reginald, Member of Parliament; former spokesman, Industrial Relations, Labour Party, 24 July 1972.

Roberts, Prof. B. C., London School of Economics and Political Science, 17 August 1972.

Scott, Nicholas, Member of Parliament, 26 July 1972.

Shanks, Michael, author; Director, BOC International; former Director-General, Social Affairs, EEC: 25 July 1969, 26 July 1972, 3 August 1977.

Shephard, Robert, Political Adviser to James Prior, Minister for Employment, 25 June 1979, 10 July 1980.

Silkin, John, Minister, Ministry of Agriculture, 15 August 1977.

Smith, Edward, Cabinet Office, 28 July 1975.

Swindon, Alan, Director, Industrial Relations, Confederation of British Industry, November 1974, 13 August 1975, 17 August 1977, etc.

Teague, Michael, Research Department, Association of Scientific, Technical and Managerial Staffs, 2 August 1972.

Thane, John, Head, Research Department, National Union of Public Employers, 23 July 1980.

Torode, John, former Labour Correspondent, *Guardian*, 23 August 1972.

Urwin, D. H., Deputy General Secretary, Transport and General Workers

Union; member, TUC General Council: 2 August 1977.

Weighell, Sidney, General Secretary, National Union of Railwaymen, 7 June 1979.

Willis, Norman, Head of Research Department, Transport and General Workers Union, now Deputy General Secretary, TUC: 7 August 1972, 18 July 1980.

Woodcock, George, former General Secretary, TUC; former Chairman, Commission on Industrial Relations: 12 July 1969, 26 July 1972, 21 August 1972, 26 July 1973.

Plus other members of the TUC staff, union leaders, politicians and civil servants who wish to remain anonymous.

Index